WILLIAM DAVISON'S
NEW SPECIMEN

WILLIAM DAVISON'S

NEW SPECIMEN OF
CAST-METAL ORNAMENTS
AND WOOD TYPES

introduced with an account of
his activities as Pharmacist and Printer
in Alnwick, 1780 - 1858

PETER ISAAC

LONDON

PRINTING HISTORICAL SOCIETY

Published by
The Printing Historical Society
St Bride Institute
Bride Lane, London EC4
© 1990
ISBN 900003 09 X
Publication No. 12
Set in 'Monotype' Bulmer by
Gloucester Typesetting Services
Printed and bound in Great Britain
by Smith Settle, Otley

CONTENTS

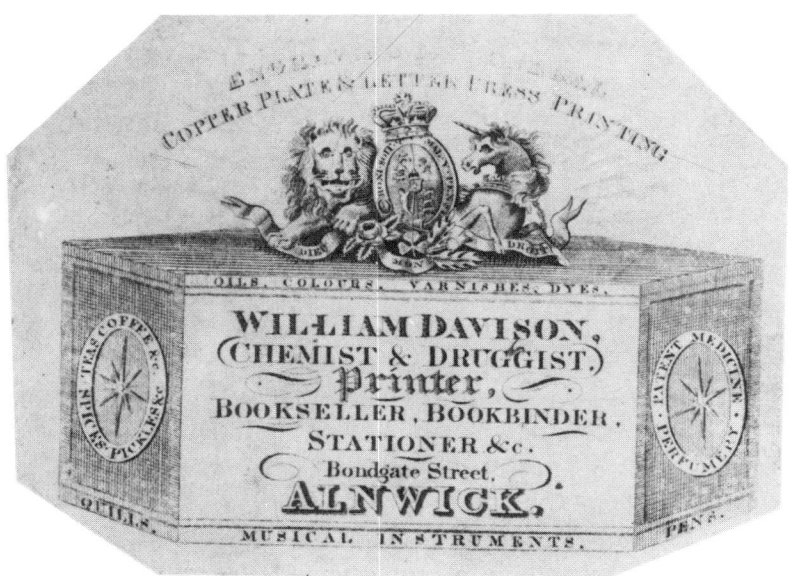

NOW THAT THE Printing Historical Society has embarked on the publication of specimen books of typefounders and printers, it seems appropriate to reproduce this very unusual specimen book put out in the early nineteenth century[1] by the enterprising Alnwick pharmacist and printer, William Davison, and to try to relate it to the printer's life and times. This revised version of a paper that I gave to the Bibliographical Society on the 17 March 1964 is, accordingly, used to introduce him and his work in the Northeast of England, an area famous also for Thomas Bewick.

William Davison was born in Newcastle upon Tyne in October 1780, being baptized in St Andrew's Church on the 22nd of that month. He was a son of John Davison, a joiner.[2] It seems likely that William started his apprenticeship with Mr Hind, a Newcastle chemist, in 1794 or 1795, because Skelly[3] reports that he 'arrived' in Alnwick in 1802 to set up business as a pharmacist. In 1803 he was, for a short time, in partnership with Joseph Perry, an Alnwick printer.[4] Davison dissolved his partnership with Perry on the 6 March 1803, but this short period in the trade seems to have given him a taste for printing. As we shall see, he later assisted John Catnach,[5] and, as a result of the latter's bankruptcy, came again into printing – and that most successfully for fifty years.

This introduction is, of course, concerned with Davison the printer, but it is worth emphasizing that, during his half-century of active printing and publishing, he was also a very active and successful pharmacist and apothecary – a common combination of trades for many years. Hindley, for example, writes[6]

> The chemistry department in Mr. Davison's establishment was noted in the North of England. As a school for the study of medicine, it was remarkable for the many eminent men that emanated from it; and it is pleasing to look back upon the names of not a few who in after life became distinguished in the various walks of science.

In particular, Davison's son, also William, was a doctor, and he is supposed to have trained under his father.

[7]

John Catnach was born in 1769 at Burntisland in Fifeshire, where his father is supposed to have owned some powder-mills. Hindley, getting a little mixed with his Christian names, suggests that Catnach was apprenticed in Edinburgh to an uncle, Alexander Robinson, a printer.[7] When out of his time John Catnach worked briefly as a journeyman in Edinburgh before moving to Berwick upon Tweed, where he started a small printing business of his own. In Berwick he married Mary Hutchinson, a native of Dundee, and there their eldest son, John, was born, dying at Alnwick five and a half years later.

In 1790 John Catnach moved his business some thirty miles south to Alnwick, where he set up his press in Narrowgate. We find in the Alnwick parish registers the record of the births of seven children to John Catnach and Mary. Amongst these was James, born on the 18 August 1792. Jemmy Catnach afterwards became famous as the Seven-Dials printer of last dying words and other lurid Victorian emphemera; but that is another story.[8]

It is clear that Catnach was a bookseller with initiative and taste, and even, it may be said, with some pretensions. Almost the earliest publication of which we know is *The Alnwick Magazine*, of which at least four numbers seem to have been issued in 1792,[9] and the next, a 94-page book, was Milton's *Paradise Regained*. An interesting sidelight on his pretensions is given by my copy of vol. ii of William Hutchinson's *View of Northumberland* (1778), to which Catnach has added a cancel title-page 'The History of the following Places in Northumberland' with a list of these, and with the imprint 'Alnwick, Sold by J. Catnach, Printer, and Stationer'. (The printer was, in fact Thomas Saint of Newcastle.) Some of his early work was of a low typographical standard, but in 1796 Catnach started to use illustrations in his work: a woodcut in a theological polemic and four copperplate engravings in an edition of Thomson's *The Seasons*. By the end of the century Catnach was aiming higher with the *Hermit of Warkworth* ('elegantly hot-pressed'), and *The Idler* and *Journey to the Western Islands* of Johnson. The earliest sure contact between Catnach and Thomas Bewick was 1792.[10]

Whether these and his other bookselling activities were more enthusiastic than businesslike, or whether, as suggested by Hindley,[11] he was unduly fond of the bottle, by 1801 he was in low financial water. We learn from a cutting from the *Newcastle Chronicle*, dated 28 November 1801, that he had assigned all his personal estate to two trustees for the benefit of his creditors.

He must have cleared his indebtedness – perhaps by borrowing adequate working capital – because the four years from 1804 are marked by a number of attractive publications, well printed and with illustrations, at least some of which were by Bewick. These include Bishop Percy's *Hermit of Warkworth* (super-royal 8°, 1805), de Buffon's *Natural History* (small 8°, 1804),[12] *Beauties of Natural History, selected from Buffon's History of Quadrupeds*, nd) etc. He was also producing the chapbooks and children's books, for which Alnwick later became famous; these include *The Royal Play Book: or Children's Friend*, *A Present for Little Masters and Misses*, *The Death and Burial of Cock Robin*. They were illustrated with woodcuts, some of which may have come from the Bewick workshop.

In 1807 he felt himself sufficiently established to take an apprentice, Mark Smith, who later became one of Alnwick's active printers. When Catnach moved to Newcastle in 1808, as we shall see, Smith's indentures were broken and he went to London to complete his apprenticeship.[13] At this time also Catnach must have been planning the editions of Burns, Beattie, and Blair which came out in 1807 and 1808, some with his imprint only and some with the joint imprint of Catnach and Davison – and this brings us to the brief Catnach-Davison partnership.

THE CATNACH–DAVISON PARTNERSHIP

We have evidence for the Catnach-Davison partnership not only in the registrations under the Seditious Societies Act 1799, but also in the joint imprints on the editions, published during 1807 and 1808, of the *Poetical Works* of Burns, Percy's *Hermit of Warkworth*, Beattie's *Minstrel*, and Blair's *The Grave*. The explanation of this somewhat strange partnership is to be found, I think, in a letter published by Burman in 1896.[14] The letter, dated 25 October 1816, from Thomas Bewick to William Davison runs

> I received your Letter inclosing your Promissory Note, at 3 months for £16. 8s. 6d. which when paid will settle your Acct. for Wood Cuts done for yourself – but you take no notice of the painful and disagreeable affair of Catnach's – you no doubt will well remember that I wou'd not trust Catnach at a 6d., neither wou'd I at all have undertaken to do the Cuts for the Hermit of Warkworth, had not you & Mr. Bell promised to pay me £25 on acct. of that publication, the Cuts for which, I understand are in your hands – The Cuts for the Hermit came to £44 13s. 8d. – of this sum I paid Mr. Craig for making the Designs £17 17s., besides (I believe) some carriage and postage; & all I got of Catnach towards payment for these Cuts was £6 10s. leaving a balance of £38 3s. 8d. – you and Mr. Bell ought in honour immediately to pay me what you have promised – you £15 & he £10, as is plainly promised in both your Letters, before I began the Cuts & in your subsequent Letters to me you also gave me to understand that what you promised you wou'd perform & I hope both you and Mr. Bell will send me your joint promissory note without delay for the above sum . . .

The letter is interesting in several respects: firstly, it shows Catnach's continuing financial embarrassment and unreliability (Mr Bell was the agent for the trustees in the assignment mentioned earlier). Secondly, it shows clearly the cost of the splendid *Hermit* wood-engravings, of which there were eleven and a cut of the Percy arms (no. 123) for the dedication to Frances Julia, Duchess of Northumberland. (These are reproduced as nos. 37–47 in the accompanying specimen book.) Thirdly, it confirms a point made to me by Mr Iain Bain, namely that Bewick seldom illustrated literary texts; it will be noticed that, in this case, he has sought the assistance of Craig for the designs, and has limited his role to the engraving of someone else's visual interpretation.

At this date we have no means of finding out why Davison was drawn to help Catnach; they were not especially close together, Davison's shop being in Bondgate Within and Catnach's printery in Narrowgate. Perhaps Davison had already extended his pharmacy to include stationery. Be that as it may, from 1807 until his death in June 1858 Davison never ceased to be a most active printer, publisher, and stationer – as well as continuing as an active pharmacist and apothecary.

Burman[15] suggests that the first-fruit of the partnership was Beattie's *The Minstrel* (super-royal 8°, 1807), and this contains an advertisement for the first part of the Catnach–Davison Burns *Poetical Works* (fcp 8°, 1807–8), which suggests that the Burns closely followed the Beattie.

[9]

Rules and Regulations

TO BE OBSERVED IN

W. DAVISON'S OFFICES,

ALNWICK.

—·······—

I. The Hours of Attendance are from Seven in the Morning until Seven in the Evening, excepting on Saturdays at Six in the Evening. One half Hour to be allowed at Nine o'Clock for Breakfast, and one Hour at One o'Clock for Dinner. And any Apprentice neglecting the Hours to make up the time deficient at other opportunities when the Overseers think proper; but no deficiency shall be allowed to be made up during the time of Candle Light.

II. None of those employed in the Offices are to Swear, or use any unbecoming Language, or make any unnecessary Noise, or prevent the other Workmen from doing their duty, on any pretence whatever.

III. When any Cases are taken out of the Racks, in the Printing Office, the Compositor is to return them into their proper place immediately after he has done with the same. Sweepings of Frames to be cleared away before One o'Clock every day, and Matter broken by accident to be cleared away on the same day. Jobs and Pie of any sort, on Boards, Windows, Frames, &c. shall be cleared away immediately after notice.

IV. When a Compositor carries his Form down for Press, he is not to put two Forms together without a Partition between them; and if, through neglect of such Partition, a Form should be battered, the Compositor guilty of such neglect shall pay the damage done to the Letter, &c.

V. The Saw, Bowl, Sponge, Letter-brush, Sheers, Knives, Bellows, &c. to be return-ed to their respective Places as soon as done with. No Person to take a Bodkin, Composing-stick, &c. not his own, without permission of the Owner, or hoard useful Sorts, not wanting or likely to want them.

VI. In the Binding Office, the Boy to have all the Hammers, Pressing-Boards, Cutting-Boards, Folders, Knives, Sheers, &c. put in their proper places previous to 7 o'Clock in the Morning.

VII. The Boy or Boys to make on the Fires when necessary, and to Sweep out the Offices previous to the Hour of 7 in the Morning, and run all Errands for the use of the same, also to see that the Fires be put out at Night. The Stairs of the Offices to be swept Month and Month about by the respective Boys.

VIII. All those employed in the Offices to put down, every Night, the work they have done through the Day in a Book kept for that purpose, which Book is to be inspected by the Overseers to prevent mistakes. And the Books of the several Offices are to be brought to the Shop every Saturday Evening for approval.

IX. Any Apprentice repeating a Fault or Neglect, shall not only make up the deficient Time, but shall work over, to make up any loss caused by such Fault or Neglect. And any Journeyman neglecting his duty in any respect whatever shall be accountable for the same.

X. If it is found necessary to borrow any article from a different Office, such article to be returned as soon as possible to the Office from which it was borrowed.

XI. The Overseers to see that the above Rules be kept in force without any di-minution whatever; and if any Overseer either refuse to pay proper attention to the Hours, or permit others in the Office to do the same, or neglect to render full Ac-counts of the transactions of the Week every Saturday Evening at Six o'Clock, he shall be discharged from his Office, and another shall be appointed in his stead.

It may be that Davison, who gives every evidence of being reliable and businesslike, soon dissolved the partnership, but we find that, in 1808, John Catnach moved from Alnwick to Newcastle, where he set up business in a small shop in Newgate Street. From this address he published a number of illustrated works, but his debts continued to grow, and in 1812 or 1813 he was again bankrupt. Just before being sent to the debtors' gaol Catnach had managed to send his wife and daughters to London, together with a wooden press and a small quantity of type. In London Mary Catnach and her daughters were assisted by Mark Smith, the former Catnach apprentice, who was then working for John Walker of Paternoster Row. Smith managed to borrow money, from another former Alnwick resident, to help Mrs Catnach and her family, and soon afterwards John Catnach arrived in London. He set up business in Wardour Street, but, returning home on the evening of the 29 August 1813, he fell and injured his leg; he was taken to St George's Hospital, where rheumatic fever supervened, and he died on the 4 December 1813.[16]

DAVISON AS A PRINTER

Davison came into printing at an opportune moment. He had been preceded in Alnwick by only five printers: T. Alder, John Catnach, J. Vint (later better known in London), J. Perry and M. & J. Graham. The beginning of the nineteenth century saw a great rise in the demand for popular printing, and chapbooks and garlands enjoyed a vogue in Scotland and northern England from about 1770 to 1830.

Hindley describes William Davison as 'by far the most enterprising printer that had settled in the North of England'.[17] This claim can be well supported not only by the richness of what we may call Davison's 'literary publications', which are listed in the accompanying checklist, but also by the diversity of his other efforts in the printing field: chapbooks and children's books, schoolbooks, billheads and commercial printing,[18] a newspaper (still in existence), prints and guide-books, cast-metal ornaments and wood-letter (the subject of the accompanying specimen book), etc. The whole adds up to a very considerable achievement for a most active pharmacist and apothecary.

It is interesting to note that, quite early in his career, Davison adopted stereotyping, although this was at the time by no means a general technique. In listing the *Hermit* cuts Hugo writes[19]

> Davison was a celebrated printer at Alnwick, and employed Thomas Bewick to illustrate his publications. He used the cuts thus obtained, and sometimes with questionable taste, in the embellishment not only of his best and choicest, but of scores of his least important and cheapest books. He rarely, however, employed his Blocks themselves, but used stereotypes of them, many of which are widely diffused among the printers of the North of England. 'The Hermit of Warkworth' is a special favourite in that part of the kingdom, and I have seen the whole of the book, engravings and letterpress, on a set of stereotype plates, which came from Davison's Printing Office.

It seems clear that Davison stereotyped for other publishers and booksellers. There are, for example, in a set of Local Tracts 'Poetry' (vol. 11) in the Newcastle upon Tyne City Library[20] two identical 24-page chapbook editions of the *Hermit*; one bears Davison's imprint, the other carries the imprint 'South Shields, Published by R. M. Kelly, Market Place'. A careful study of damaged letters, etc., shows these two editions to be identical except for the imprints.

NEW

SPECIMEN

OF

CAST METAL

ORNAMENTS

AND

WOOD TYPES,

SOLD BY

W. DAVISON,

ALNWICK.

Skelly, whose dates cannot always be relied upon, writes[21]

It was somewhat about the year 1814 that he established a small foundry on his premises in Bondgate for the production of metal stereotypes, and it would be about this time where he says that he paid Thomas Bewick as much as £500 for wood engravings; the magnificent trade catalogue that he issued, and which contains upwards of eleven hundred specimens of engravings, will ever form an undying monument of the zeal and energy of this enterprising man.[22]

This brings us to the attractive specimen book that the Society is reprinting for its double interest as an unusual example of the enterprise of a provincial printer and because of its Bewick association. It contains a total of 1082 impressions of wood-engravings, stock cuts, metal ornaments, wood letters, ornamental borders, etc. It is printed on one side only of 130 leaves of a white wove paper of no outstanding quality (but presumably of rag furnish). There are, as the reader may see, one or two duplicate impressions. It usually bears a tipped-in title-page 'NEW SPECIMEN OF CAST-METAL ORNAMENTS AND WOOD TYPES, SOLD BY W. DAVISON, ALNWICK.', within a border made up of units, some at least of which may be seen in the nineteenth-century founders' catalogues. As you may see, each line of the title is in a different size and face. My copy of this specimen book has a title-page different from the others that I have seen; it is reproduced here for comparison.

This specimen book is difficult to date, but it seems likely that it was printed at more than one date.[23] The royal arms nos. 109–122, having the arms of Hanover in the middle of the shield place the date of these before the accession of Victoria in 1837. Cut no. 114 must date from 1820 or later, and cut no. 951 from 1830 or later, and no. 947, on the same leaf, from before 1837. On the other hand the attractive cut of Sunderland bridge and harbour breakwater (no. 1004) is clearly Victorian. While it is perhaps easier to imagine that Davison issued the specimen at one time – and that after 1837 – evidence for issue 'in parts' is given by a very battered copy of the cuts nos. 925–1100, together with the title-page which is detached, in the John Johnson Collection in the Bodleian Library; this collection also has two copies of the complete specimen. These cuts may have been the second part referred to by Skelly, and may have been the occasion of the publication of the title-page.

A second question that anyone looking at the specimen book must ask is whether the cuts were printed from the originals or from stereotypes made from them. It is difficult to believe that there was such a demand for the blocks[24] that Davison made stereos from the whole of his large stock of cuts; it seems more likely that he stereotyped the cuts to order. Nor does the fact that one or two of the cuts are duplicated weaken this view, since the specimen consists of separate leaves, which would have been printed in breaks in the normal work of the shop. Hugo, in his *Bewick Collector*, is very indecisive on this matter.[25]

In most of the copies that I have seen some 400 of the cuts are marked 'Bewick' by a stamp or with a manuscript 'B', intended to indicate that these cuts are by Bewick or come from his workshop. Iain Bain doubts the claim, and discusses it in the next section, which he has completely rewritten from my original paper. The first forty-nine cuts illustrate the Burns, Beattie, Blair, and Fergusson poetical works, and the *Hermit*. I suspect that the attribution to Bewick was made later in the nineteenth century, when, under the influence of the Revd Thomas Hugo, almost any illustration on wood was attributed to the Newcastle wood-engraver. Davison used his cuts in many situations from halfpenny chapbooks to the elegant poets.

Nevertheless, the fact that the printer was offering the large *Hermit* cuts (nos. 39, 44 and 47) for sale at as little as 15*s*. each, offers strong confirmation of Hugo's belief that Davison had made stereotype copies of them.[26] There are also many stock cuts for tea (with the then customary Chinese figures), tobacco (with the usual Red Indian), auctions, race cards, walking stallions, royal arms, Newcastle arms, etc. Strangely, at least nine of the cuts contain the name 'Smith, Printer',[27] in some cases partly erased (see nos. 57, 59, 61, 72 – one of my favourites – 76, 78, 80, 82 and 84). Another, no. 860, bears the signature of the London engraver and punch cutter Richard Austin, and nos. 135, 136, 139, 935, 991 and 1098 are shown in the recently discovered specimen book of Louis Jean Pouchée referred to by James Mosley in his note on p. 39. It would seem that Davison was not above buying up the stock of other printers to stereotype,[28] as well as ready-made material from other founders. At least three stereotypes of tail-pieces from the *Burns* have survived in private collections – nos. 166, 174 and 248. It is plain that they have been made from the original woodblocks for they reproduce the locally lowered surfaces so typical of Bewick's workshop. Original woodblocks for nos. 2, 20, 27, 28, 452, and 960 also survive in private collections. We have no idea how widely Davison's stereotypes were distributed over the Northeast of England, but the extent and elegance of the accompanying specimen book suggests that they must have made a contribution to the expansion of printing in the area.

DAVISON AND BEWICK

To some extent Davison's wider reputation has rested on his connection with Thomas Bewick and the Newcastle engraving shop. That there was considerable contact between them there is no doubt, but like so many other areas of the engraver's story, the extent of the connection has been exaggerated by the optimistic enthusiasm generated by the nineteenth-century collectors such as Hugo and Burman. The facts presented by Bewick's own records, now preserved in the Tyne & Wear Archives Service, show that between 1802 and 1813 approximately 102 blocks were engraved at a total cost of £104 19*s*. 6*d*., at prices ranging from three guineas to two shillings. So much for the 'near 500 woodcuts by Bewick' later advertised in the sale catalogue of Davison's effects. In this context it is also important to remember that after Bewick's partnership with his former master Ralph Beilby ended in 1797, the amount of wood engraving he worked on himself, for anything other than his own books of natural history, was very small indeed.

As already noted most known copies of the Davison specimen book show many cuts identified with the letter B for Bewick, either stamped with type or written by hand, very likely at a time after Davison's death and perhaps concurrently. The largest group thus marked, nos. 361–753 were for the most part engraved for the Buffon *Natural History* of 1814, and although many have been inspired by Bewick's work – similar attitudes are laterally reversed – they are from another hand altogether. Apart from there being no record of such a series being cut, a letter from Davison to Bewick of 11 May 1813 'respecting the copying of Animals from your History' continues

I do assure you I never Intended it or neither had I any Idea that such a thing was done Indeed my express orders were that none of them should be taken from any other Persons Works but from Drawings of the Persons Own to be taken from Nature if Possible therefore If I am led into any error you may rely on it I had no intention or I trust never will of Attempting to take any Persons right whether Copyright or Otherwise . . .[29]

It is extremely unlikely that Bewick ever visited Alnwick specifically to work on cuts for Davison, as reported by Burman.[30] We do know from an annotated proof of an engraving of Bamburgh Castle that Davison at some time 'kept an engraver on wood'[31] which presumably means employed him on his own premises. There is a possibility that some of the Buffon cuts were the work of Bewick's apprentice Isaac Nicholson who by 1811 was out of his time and working on his own account in Newcastle.

The Davison books actually identified in Bewick's accounts are the *Hermit of Warkworth* (commissioned by Catnach in 1805), Burns's *Poems*, 1807–9, and Ferguson's *Poems*, 1811–13. The earliest commission from Davison appears to be a cut of 'Glauber's Head': delivered 18 September 1802 presumably for the labelling of a salts bottle. Two other jobbing items of this earlier period were a 'card cut', 30 July 1803 and a 'facsimile on wood' 22 November 1805.

Davison used the tail-piece blocks for Burns's *Poems* in a good deal of other work and a number reappear in Fergusson's *Poems* and in the Buffon *Natural History*. There is little doubt that stereotypes were used. One or two of them, nos. 174, 208 and 233 in particular, are very close to Bewick's manner, which cannot be said of the principal cuts for the two verse collections which are also strongly influenced by the style of the draughtsman John Thurston. Some of the tail-pieces, such as nos. 204 and 231 show the hand of Isaac Nicholson as seen in the many vignettes he produced for Emerson Charnley's *Fishers' Garlands* of the 1820s.

The last contact between Davison and Bewick's workshop so far discovered is seen in a letter written from Alnwick in May 1818 in which Davison enclosed the work of a London engraver which he wanted done in Newcastle provided he could get an equally low price. Intended for a children's book, Bewick priced them at 3s. 6d. or 4s. for the small, and 7s. 6d. for the larger, but no record exists of the work's being carried out.[32]

DAVISON'S BOOKS

An analysis of Davison's more substantial publications is illuminating; almost two-thirds fall into two categories – verse and school-books (including books of reference). If we include natural history with the second category, we are left with local guides and histories, local authors, and a miscellaneous collection including theology. This analysis helps us to understand Davison's publishing motives – we shall return to this later in discussing the *Alnwick Mercury*. We can see that the printer was intent on bringing to a wide public, and in an attractive form, the 'standard' poets of the day, and on providing good, inexpensive school-books. He gave good support to local authors and he was concerned to record the history of his own town. Naturally he was drawn into the local debates and some of his theological works reflect this.

From Catnach Davison took over the two-volume Burns (fcp 8°, 1807), Blair's *The Grave* (1808), Beattie's *The Minstrel* (fcp 8°, 1807) and Percy's *Hermit of Warkworth* (crown 4°, 1807).[33] Each of

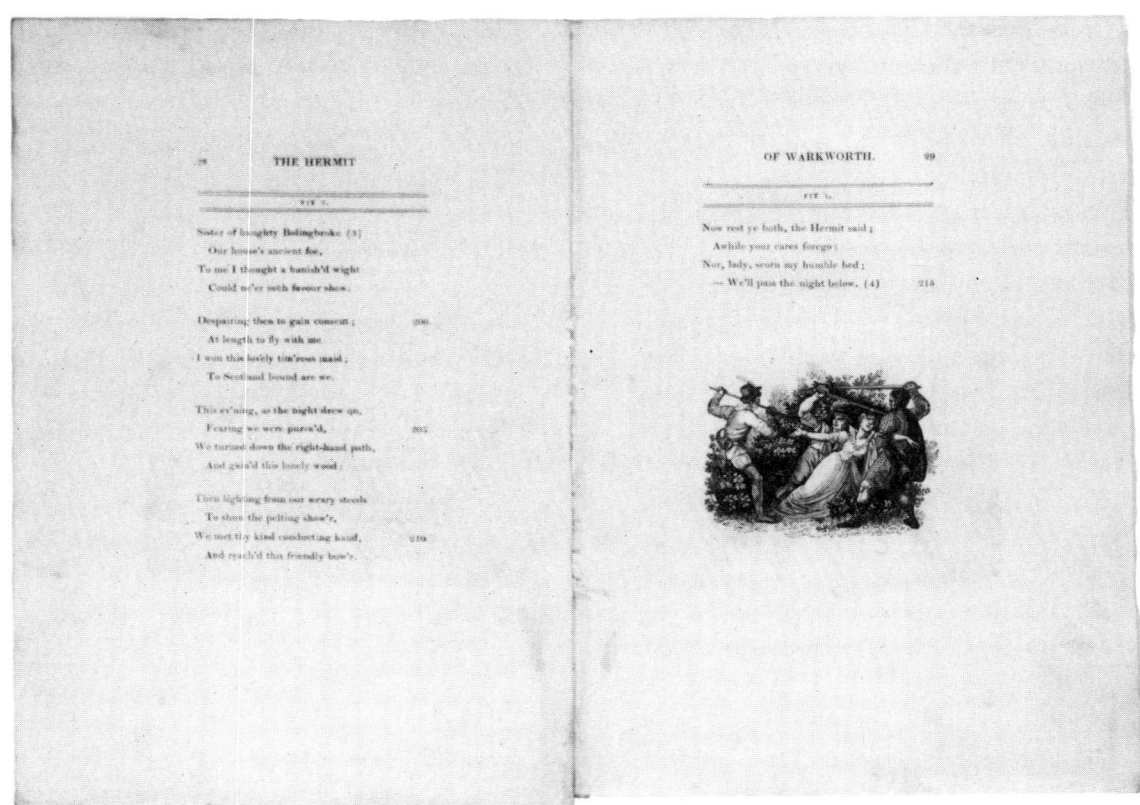

The Hermit of Warkworth, Alnwick, 1805. 240 × 170mm.

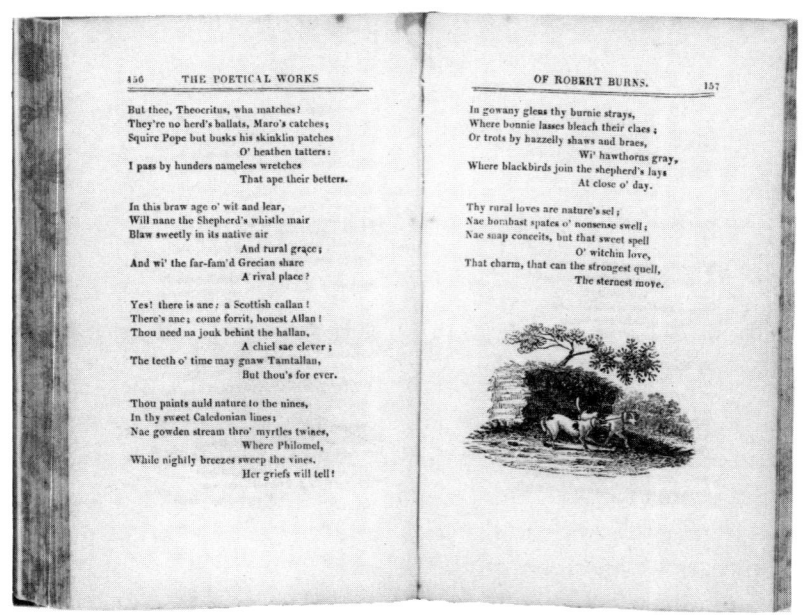

Burns's *Poems*, Alnwick, 1814. 161 × 95mm.

[16]

these well-presented works is illustrated with wood-engravings. (Indeed, a comparison of the illustrations with those displayed in the accompanying specimen shows that at least seventy-three of Davison's large stock of wood-engravings were taken over from Catnach.)

It is difficult to offer any solidly based bibliographical evidence about these early works – or, indeed, about many of Davison's publications; they are no longer commonly met with and too often dated letterpress title-pages have been replaced by engraved titles, which were clearly used for several editions. This is demonstrated, for example, in the Burns, where it is not uncommon to find the engraved title-page bearing Davison's imprint with a text that carries that of Catnach and Davison. Clearly Burns was a popular poet in Northumberland in the first quarter of the nineteenth century, and it is possible to differentiate at least four Davison editions between 1808 and 1828. C. C. Burman, indeed, lists three editions by Catnach and Davison, and thirteen by Davison alone, over the same period. Even more popular, on the evidence of distinguishable editions, was Percy's *Hermit of Warkworth*. Here there are eight distinct editions between 1807 and 1850; some of the early editions had large-paper (4°) issues as well as the smaller format more usual for Davison. There was also an unusual edition (crown 12°, 1841) 'adapted for theatrical representation' by Robert Wilkie.[34]

These 'standard' poets cost 5s. to 8s. per volume in boards. Usually even less expensive were several of the local authors. These included

a. Thomas Adams, *Poetical Works* (fcp 8°, 1811)
b. Robert Anderson, *Ballads in the Cumberland Dialect* (roy 32°, nd)
c. Thomas Donaldson, *Poems, chiefly in the Scottish Dialect* (demy 12°, 1809)
d. Isabella Hindmarsh, *The Cave of Hoonga* (fcp 8°, 1818)
e. J. L. Luckley, *The Pleasures of Sight* (demy 12°, 1847, 2 editions)
f. William Probert, *The Gododin*, translated from the Welsh (post 8°, nd)
g. James Service, *The Wandering Knight of Dunstanburgh Castle* (fcp 8°, 1822)
h. —— *Metrical Legends of Northumberland* (demy 12°, 1834)

On the whole Davison put out these authors in a sufficiently handsome style; for example, the Adams, with its wood-engraved vignettes and engraved frontispiece, is in no wise inferior to the Burns.

Three prose works by local authors are also worthy of notice; these are

i. William Forrester Bow, *Notions of the Nature of Fever, and of Nervous Action* (demy 8°, 1829). Bow is known for his eponymous liniment.[35]
ii. W. H. Brown, *Journal of a Voyage from London to Barbadoes* (fcp 8°, 1836)
iii. Thomas Sopwith, *Account of the Mining Districts of Alston Moor* (demy 12°, 1833)

Davison produced short histories of Alnwick and guides to the town and castle. The substantial *History* (demy 8°, 2nd ed., 1822) is a notable effort and worthy to take its place alongside Tate's well-known history. It seems to have been almost all that came of Davison's projected history of Northumberland. In January 1820 he put out an eight-page advertisement about this, stating that for the previous four years he had been engaged in collecting and arranging materials. To extend his information he included a five-page questionary containing seventy questions relating to antiquities, biography, natural history, agriculture, trade, population, etc. He also gave the information that the history was to be published in parts on fine demy paper at 5s. each, or on Whatman's Royal Drawing paper, with proof impressions of the plates at 10s. 6d. each. (Incidentally, it is appropriate to observe that the Alnwick *History* was published in four parts (demy 8°) at 2s. each, or 4s. each for the superior issue.) Skelly[36] tells us that the Alnwick *History* was written by Davison himself with the assistance of A. H. Tate, his foreman, the Revd William Probert, and Andrew Wright.[37] No doubt these same three coadjutors assisted him in the preparatory work on the larger history. In the course of this preparation Davison had a large number of plates engraved of places of interest in the county, and, as we shall see, these were later sold as separate plates. Now scarce, they may occasionally be found in grangerized copies of Hodgson's or Mackenzie's Histories of Northumberland. It was, indeed, the publication of these latter works in the years 1820 to 1835 that cut the ground from under Davison's feet.

Another book with its own story is the *Life of James Allan, the Celebrated Northumbrian Piper* (crown 8°, 1818). On the title-page this bears the imprint 'Printed and published by W Guthrie, Blyth', but Davison's imprint is to be found on p. 384. In my grangerized copy of Burman's earlier work[38] there is a transcription in Dr Burman's hand of a letter from Mackenzie and Dent to D. W. Smith, of Alnwick, explaining why there were two rather similar editions in 1818 of this work: Guthrie's and their own.

> Andrew Wight of North Shields, who is foreman to Mr Appleby Printer, is the writer of Allan's Life; and in order to encourage a young man named Guthrie who commenced the Printing business at Blyth we gave him part of the MSS and agreed that the book should be printed for their mutual benefit.

Guthrie then intended to enter the work at Stationers' Hall when he had the whole manuscript. Wight becoming alarmed finally sold his copyright to Mackenzie and Dent who agreed to publish it. At the same time Davison agreed with Guthrie to publish the work, which had presumably been at least partly printed by Guthrie. This all seems rather odd and the book can have had only a fairly limited demand, though the Newcastle edition is by no means scarce.

In 1882 there were at least six 'public' schools in Alnwick – the Duke's and the Duchess's Schools for poor boys and poor girls, and the Freeman's Schools (Grammar, English, Forster, and Girls')[39] – and several 'reputable private schools'. There was, therefore, it may be surmised, a steady market for school-books, and this Davison seems to have met. Perhaps his most successful school-book was an edition of Charles Hutton's *Complete Treatise on Practical Arithmetic and Book-keeping* (demy 12°, 1828) corrected and enlarged by James Ferguson, a schoolmaster in the Freemen's Schools. This work carries the note 'Price 2s. 6d. Bound – Liberal allowance to schools.' Skelly[40] writes

> In the cause of education Mr Davison was unsparing in his efforts, and this will be seen, not only in the large number of books that he published for educational purposes, but more especially in that particular class of literature, known as 'Children's Books'.

Perhaps the most noteworthy of his children's books were the four-volume de Buffon (tcp 8°, 1814), and the little *Natural History of British Quadrupeds* etc. (fcp 12°, 1809 [?1819]).[41] The latter was made up from seven chapbooks, but it was also published consecutively paginated in at least two other editions in the same small format. Many of the rather delicate wood-engravings, copied from the Bewick workshop, are found in all these natural-history books, and the great majority are found in the accompanying specimen book.

The first years of the nineteenth century seem to have produced a great deal of religious dissension in Alnwick. About 1820 a splinter group from the Methodists became first Arminians and then Unitarians. This gave rise to several books, of which I have seen Crozer's *Alnwick Unitarian Debate* (demy 12°, 2nd ed., 1826), and Hyndman's *Lectures on the Principles of Unitarianism* (roy 18°, 1824). Neither is a particularly sparkling piece of printing.

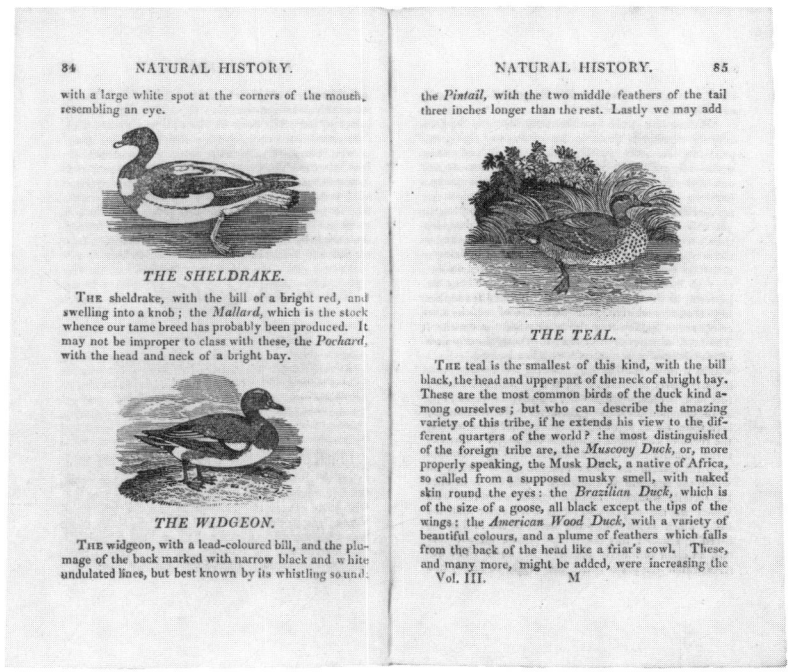

de Buffon's *System of Natural History*, Vol. 3, Alnwick, 1814. 155 × 91mm.

DAVISON'S PRAYER BOOK AND BIBLE

Very different, however, are Davison's splendid octavo *Book of Common Prayer* (demy 8°, 1817) and *Universal Holy Bible; or Complete Library of Divine Knowledge* (demy f°, 2 vols, nd [*c* 1820]).[42] The prayer book is an excellent piece of book-making and is accompanied by the metrical psalms in the version of Tate and Brady. There is an engraved frontispiece and four plates in the text, engraved by E. Mitchell. In particular the plate of 'burial of the dead' shows Alnwick Parish Church of St Michael across the adjoining graveyard. Skelly writes[43]: 'The size of the Prayer Book was greatly against it ever becoming generally used by the regular churchgoer, but as a work of merit it reflects highly upon the press from whence it emanated.' The type is attractively large (English or, say, 14 pt) with bourgeois or long primer for the rubrics and footnotes. It would serve excellently as an altar book.

Even more startling as the production of a small provincial press is the folio Bible. Its full title is *The Universal Holy Bible; or Complete Library of Divine Knowledge; containing the Sacred Text . . . with marginal references . . .* (2 vols, demy f° in 4s, 1820 on letterpress title of New Testament). Presumably the extensive footnotes, which take up at least one-third of the space, take the work out of the perpetual copyright of the Queen's Printers and of the two University Presses. In his preface the editor writes

> To explain and illustrate the Sacred Scriptures, the labours of many truly great, and eminently pious men have been directed, but many of which are so voluminous, and of course so expensive as to render them inaccessible to the generality of readers; for which reason, the object of the present edition is to form a judicious selection from the deservedly popular and highly esteemed authors; by carefully comparing them together, to unite the excellencies, and most striking beauties of the whole, without injury to the sense of either; and by connecting them, to form a complete summary of scripture doctrines and history, with suitable and practical reflections to which they give rise.

Once again, it is clear, Davison was making more widely available an essential and scholarly work.

The typographical appearance is simple. The Bible is printed in two columns separated by a double rule. The title of the book and a running head, enclosed in thick-and-thin double rules, runs across the top of each page. There are marginal references in nonpareil. The text type is a somewhat aggressively modern face in great primer (say 18 pt). About one-third of each page is occupied by commentary, which is set in two columns, of wider measure than the text; the type is a modern face in long primer. In all there are forty-nine engraved plates.

The Bible was published in 100 parts at 1s. each.[44] It was clearly no financial success, and we can still find it advertised in the *Alnwick Mercury* of 1 November 1859, nearly eighteen months after Davison's death; it was then priced at 26s. In Skelly's manuscript notebooks[45] there is a long note, not in Skelly's hand and supposedly signed 'Thos Arkle, 17 Feb 1883', which says

> I have heard that this work landed Mr Davison in great difficulties – that the publication of the Bible was slow, & that one estate he had at Woodburn Park . . . had to be sold to secure its completion. It was certainly a great undertaking for a local publisher.

Two of the three copies of this Bible that I have seen were serviceably bound in reversed calf with a simple design blind-tooled on the top and bottom covers using a roll. The copy in the University Library, Newcastle upon Tyne, whose two volumes are separate, was, I believe, bound by Davison, since both volumes carry his very attractive engraved trade-plate 'William Davison, Chemist & Druggist, Printer, Bookseller, Bookbinder, Stationers &c. Bondgate Street, Alnwick'.

CHAPBOOKS AND BATTLEDORES

> It would require a huge volume to do justice to the energy and industry of Mr Davison: he delighted equally as much in catering to the joy and amusement of young minds as in supplying of those richer stores of knowledge for the student and more advanced readers. Who, amongst us, but what has been delighted in glancing over those pretty children's books which Hugo has characterized as 'being far in advance of anything published previous to Davison's time'.

So wrote Skelly,[46] and he might legitimately have added that though they represent the popular

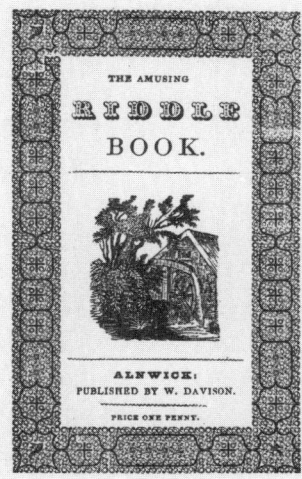

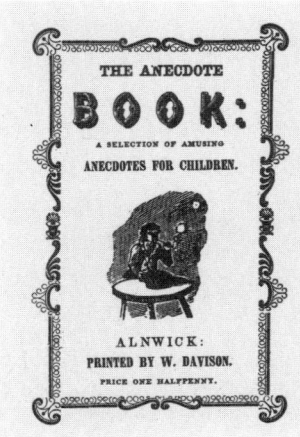

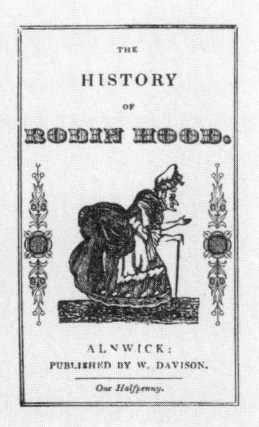

reading of their time they are as different from the lurid Seven-Dials productions as it is possible to imagine; some of them, indeed, are perhaps too ostentatiously 'improving'.

We have not space here to do more than instance one or two of these publications as examples of a class of printed material for which Northumberland was justly known in the early years of the nineteenth century.[47] As an example of the royal 32° eight-page chapbooks for children we may take *The Anecdote Book* which starts with a suitably uplifting example on the fruits of industry. These little halfpenny books were printed four-up, and are bound both with and without printed coloured-paper covers. *Tom Thumb's Play Book* (demy 18°, 36 pp. including the covers) is 'to teach children their letters, by a new and pleasant method'. This, and several of the chapbooks, are plainly shown on the cover and title-page as having been stereotyped. Printed in a fairly aggressive modern face this little book starts with various alphabets and then syllables, short words, and sentences. Finally, there are a few paragraphs illustrated by 'well made' wood-engravings – in all, a good twopennyworth. Also in royal 32° is *Songs, Divine and Moral for the use*

[21]

Alnwick
Northumberland
ENTERTAINING

Entrance to Alnwick Castle.

THE
Mercury
Advertiser, and
MISCELLANY.

No. 1.—Vol. I.]   PRINTED AND PUBLISHED BY W. DAVISON, ALNWICK, JUNE 1st, 1854.   [Price One Penny.

ADDRESS TO OUR FRIENDS.

In presenting our little Miscellany "The Alnwick Mercury" to the public, a brief notice as to our views and intentions will not be out of place.

The growing commercial importance of the country, and the constantly augmenting business transactions of the age, render a vast amount of advertisements—and of mediums for advertising—more and more necessary; and it is now generally acknowledged that the outlay of capital in this respect is ultimately a positive source of profit.

With a prevailing love of business, and active attention to its requirements, it is now not deemed impossible to combine a full appreciation of literature; and the mutual growth of these two qualities has of late been marked and rapid. It is the task of Progress, and of the Press, to foster and promote these salutary features of the times; and the facilities for advertising lately given by the legislature in the repeal of the duty, enable us not only to unite the pursuit of business with the culture of the mind, but to present our Sheet to the public on more liberal terms than if those taxes still pressed upon the community.

Our pages will be enriched with gems of literature of a miscellaneous, but instructive and entertaining character; and with the thoughts and sayings of great men will be given, from time to time, columns of entirely original and valuable matter.

The elevation of the masses, and the amelioration of their condition, it is true, has been the avowed promise and pursuit of a large number of the periodicals which constantly appear and disappear with every succeeding month. But the proposed mission—than which none can be more admirable—has too often failed—not because there is no need for such attempts, but because political, rather than social evils, have been arrayed and enquired into. Reform, and the secret of its ultimate success, lies with ourselves—at our own hearths—with the education of our own minds.

All that relates to Home comfort and Domestic economy, or which tends to promote the happiness of the Fireside, will be fully treated of and considered: matters which we confidently hope will meet with a cordial reception by our readers.

of Children by Isaac Watts (32 pp. in printed coloured-paper covers). This contains a number of hymns and is illustrated with very crude woodcuts. On its back cover is a list of twenty-six juvenile books at twopence each.

We have previously mentioned the seven natural-history chapbooks, for which there were at least two 'bogus' alternative combined title-pages. Of similar format (demy 18°, 36 pp., price 6*d.*) is *Day, a Pastoral*, a delightful little book of verse, illustrated by thirty-two engravings, those for the morning, noon and evening being particularly attractive. This may not be primarily intended for children. There were several chapbook editions of Percy's *Hermit of Warkworth*, and these and some others, e.g. *The History of Crazy Jane* (demy 18°, 1818, 6*d.*) and Allan Ramsay's *Gentle Shepherd* (demy 18°, 60 pp., 6*d.*) are almost too elegant to be described as chapbooks.

Davison also produced a number of garlands and song-books. As examples we may mention *Excellent New Songs no 11* (fcp 8°, 8 pp.) and *The Omnibus Songster* (crown 12°, 24 pp.); the latter celebrated the inauguration of the Shields-Newcastle omnibus about the year 1832.

Finally we must glance at the battledores: *The British Battledore, The Child's Battledore, New Battledore, Youth's Battledore, English Battledore* etc. Each of these is made of folded card, apparently pasted-up by the printer and each carries woodcuts and or type ornaments. They sold at 1*d.*

THE ALNWICK MERCURY

On 15 June 1855 the stamp duty on newspapers was finally repealed. A year earlier, on 1 June 1854, William Davison, already seventy-three, published the first number of the *Alnwick Mercury, Northumberland Advertiser, and Entertaining Miscellany.* The first issue, of which 1000 were printed, ran to twelve pages crown folio, and cost 1*d.* In his 'Address to Our Friends' the publisher thus explained his new venture[48]

> The growing commercial importance of the country, and the constantly augmenting business transactions of the age, render a vast amount of advertisements – and of mediums for advertising – more and more necessary . . .
>
> Our pages will be enriched with gems of literature of a miscellaneous, but instructive and entertaining character . . .
>
> The elevation of the masses, and the amelioration of their condition . . . has been the avowed promise and pursuit of a large number of the periodicals which constantly appear and disappear with every succeeding month. But the proposed mission . . . has too often failed . . . because political, rather than social evils, have been arrayed and enquired into. Reform, and the secret of its ultimate success, lies with ourselves . . . with the education of our own minds.

It seems to me that this typical nineteenth-century sentiment, combining profit and uplift, underlies the whole of Davison's printed output. Even the ephemeral is good of its kind.

Burman says that four pages of each issue were printed in London, and also tells us that J. A. H. Tate, son of Davison's foreman, was the editor.[49] Skelly, however, says that Davison retained editorial control in his own hands, while J. A. H. Tate supervised the printing.[50] Examination of the early issues certainly supports Burman's view that some, at least, of the pages were printed elsewhere. For example, in the first number pp. 2–4 and 6–11 appear typographically unlike Davison's

work with pearl and nonpareil type; in particular pp. 6–8 give a detailed 'Account of the New Crystal Palace, Sydenham' with a full-page illustration. Two of the four centre pages are labelled 'Supplement' and it may be to these that Burman was referring, but one of them is clearly printed by Davison: indeed two of the three columns are filled by an advertisement for his new publication in parts 'A Complete Repository of Scottish Strathspeys' selected by Thomas Thompson (each number 3*d*.). I have never seen this work.

In the issue for 1 December 1854 Davison tells us that he had 700 subscribers for the *Mercury* before it went to press, and that the whole edition of 1000 was sold. The number printed and the number of subscribers rose steadily, and by the time of Davison's death the monthly printing was over 2600. This seems a very substantial achievement for the time.

The *Mercury* is fascinating, not only for its local news, but also for the advertisements of local tradesmen. The advertising rate was 'Four lines, and under, (Long Primer size) One Shilling. Each additional line, One Penny.' At the same time we find that Betts's Patent Brandy cost 16*s*. per gallon and Fine Matured Glenlivet Whisky, 15*s*. per gallon! Davison was able to illustrate many of the advertisements and most of the locally contributed articles from his vast stock of ornaments and engravings. For example, the regular Railway Time Table is brought to one's immediate notice by the little cut of an early engine, tender and coach.[51]

At Davison's death his business passed to his son, Dr William Davison, who kept the paper going for about a year before selling it to Henry Hunter Blair. On 1 November 1859 it was enlarged to royal f°. Finally in 1884 it amalgamated with the *Alnwick County Gazette*, and is now published weekly as the *Northumberland Gazette*.

PRINTS, CARICATURES, ETC

Davison published a large number of intaglio plates of all sizes from a few inches square to the three engravings (20 × 16 in.) of Alnwick Castle, Dilston Hall and Prudhoe Castle.[52] Some of these we have already noticed as illustrations prepared for his projected history of Northumberland; these were issued as plates 8 × 6½ in. Others were actually used as illustrations, for example in his *History of Alnwick* and in the folio Bible. There seems no reason to doubt that Davison printed them himself, especially since the catalogue of the auction of his equipment specifically mentions copperplates.[53] It appears possible that he also published such plates quite independently of any intention to use them as illustrations. One set of such plates, for example, 'now publishing' is 'a series of picturesque miniature Views of Churches in the Diocese of Durham', which was 'patronized by the Lord Bishop of Durham'. These were the picture postcards of the period being 'printed on superfine wove Cards at 4*d*. each'.[52]

Rather more than half of the forty-nine plates in the Bible were also prepared as Chimney Ornaments, at prices ranging from 1*s*. 6*d*. for two figures (e.g. Abraham offering up Isaac) to 3*s*. each 'with Trees' (e.g. David receiving the offerings of Abigail). Many of the miniature views were also used for 'embellished note paper', a more general forerunner of the picture postcard. These were priced at 6*d*. and 8*d*. per quire of twenty-four sheets.[54]

All this is rather serious, but Davison also catered for the visual humour of his day with a series of amusing and rather crudely drawn copperplate caricatures. There were over forty of these with

THE POLITICIAN.

Printed and Published by W. Davison Alnwick.

36

LAPLANDERS

ENGLISH

AMERICANS

AFRICANS

CHINESE

HOTTENTOTS

Printed and Published by W. Davison Alnwick.

a plate size of about 9 × 6½ in. The drawings are somewhat in the style of, and often copied from, Gilray, Bunbury, Hogarth and Rowlandson. For the most part they were printed in black on a wove paper of no outstanding quality. They were also occasionally printed in vermilion and, less commonly, in terracotta. They are occasionally found hand-coloured, but it is not clear that the publisher was responsible for this. Laid paper was not uncommonly used. No individual caricature carries a complete watermark, but most of those that I have seen with a watermark have about half of the watermark 'RC' (in open characters) over the date, the dates ranging from 1812 to 1817 – 1816 is the commonest date that I have seen.[55]

DAVISON AND PUBLIC AFFAIRS

William Davison illustrates that oft-repeated maxim that the busy man can always find time to do something important. His thriving printing business and pharmacy brought him into the public life of Alnwick, and we find him taking a full part in this. In this essentially bibliographical context we can glance at only a few of the aspects of Davison as a man of affairs.

Although his father may have been a Dissenter we find that, by 1810, our printer was a church-warden,[56] being among those responsible for the erection of a workhouse in that year. Towards the end of 1815 the Alnwick Dispensary was founded 'for the prompt and judicious aid of medicines and medical advice to the indigent sick'. Initially Dr Bow, previously mentioned, was one of the physicians and Davison was apothecary.[57] Later Davison is found as a regular subscriber to the Dispensary, with Thomas Hood as the apothecary.[58] In November 1836 he stood for election as a Guardian.[59] Hindley writes[60] 'In politics Mr Davison was what is now termed a Liberal; he had strong leanings to what was then known as the Progressive School. He took a great interest in the several contests in the county that occurred during his lifetime . . .' A glance through the John Johnson and Alnwick UDC Collections shows how the various Alnwick printers were drawn into the political arguments of the time, not least Davison himself. He was, also, a supporter of any measures that would help his home-town.[61] In addition to supporting the Dispensary we find him subscribing to the Alnwick Scientific and Mechanical Institution which was founded in 1824.

Finally, as an example of his generous mind, we may quote a few passages from his *Alnwick Review* (no. 1, 18 June 1827), in which, according to Burman,[62] he is attacking the *Alnwick Quarto* and its editor-publisher, T. H. Bell.

> It has ever been the mania and plague of small towns, that their inhabitants are voraciously fond of news; and tales of the marvellous, or of the petty scandal, are swallowed with peculiar avidity. In such places, human nature appears in a very unamiable point of view. The inhabitants, for want of employment, seem like spies upon each other, and every one knows his neighbour's affairs better than his own . . .
>
> . . . for it will generally be found, with few exceptions, that the best-hearted and most worthy and honourable individuals, are those who . . . charitably imitate the humane treatment of our Saviour to the poor erring female, when . . . he told her to 'go and sin no more; for he did not condemn her . . .'
>
> . . . It appears that we have now got a *spy* upon society . . . and who (though himself addicted to low and sensual pursuits and filthy gratifications) is a *publisher* of the failings and *faux pas* of others.

[27]

In his *Mercury*, nearly thirty years later, Davison eschewed this kind of local scandal and concentrated on the more noteworthy aspects of the news.

I have not been able to trace any portrait of our subject, but, after living with Davison's work for a quarter-century, I have a mental picture of a very vigorous, able and forthright provincial tradesman, of kindly heart and liberal outlook, and with the generous nineteenth-century belief in the ameliorability of human nature, especially through education.

NOTES

1. Its possible date is discussed later.

2. In my published paper I gave his place of birth as Alnwick, and the date as November 1781. A William Davison was baptized in St Mary's Church, Alnwick, on the 16 November 1781, and there were many Davisons in that town. On the other hand, the Revd George Harris, a Unitarian Minister in Newcastle, in a notice prefacing the sermon which he preached at Davison's funeral in Alnwick on the 2 July 1858 (published as a supplement to the *Alnwick Mercury* for Monday the 2 August 1858), gives Newcastle as his place of birth, and reinforces this with the statement that the printer was a freeman of that town. This makes more explicable his apprenticeship to a Newcastle pharmacist.

3. George Skelly, *Alnwick in the Past* (Alnwick, 1896), p. 12.

4. Notice of printing presses, as required by the Seditious Societies Act 1799, in the Northumberland County Record Office (ref. QRSp 5).

5. Catnach and Davison registered their press on the 15 March 1807, and Davison alone registered his on the 19 May 1808 (Northumberland Record Office QRSp 6 & 7).

6. Charles Hindley, *The Life and Times of James Catnach* (London, 1878), p. 17.

7. Hindley, *James Catnach*, p. 2.

8. See especially Hindley, *James Catnach* and the same author's *History of the Catnach Press* (London, 1886).

9. C. C. Burman, 'An account of the art of typography as practised in Alnwick from 1748 to 1900', *History of the Berwickshire Naturalists' Club*, vol. 23 (1917), pp. 305–59.

10. The Weekly Engraving Books of the Bewick workshop record the engraving of '13 cuts' for 19s. 6d., 16 July 1792; on 6 August 1792: '9 small cuts', 2s. each, for 'Riddle Books' and 7 for 'Haymakers'.

11. *James Catnach*, p. 4.

12. Mr Iain Bain's study of the Bewick workshop records show that the cuts for this work were engraved between March 1799 and September 1800.

13. Hindley, *James Catnach*, pp. 16 & 24.

14. C. C. Burman, *An Account of the Art of Typography, as practised in Alnwick from 1781 to 1815* (Alnwick, 1896), facing p. 32. The original of this letter is in the University Library, Newcastle upon Tyne.

15. The same, p. 38.

16. Hindley, *James Catnach*, pp. 29–31.

17. *History*, p. 15.

18. There is, in the Northumberland County Record Office, a collection of over 4500 individual items. This collection formed part of Davison's file of his commercial printing. Most of the items give the name of the customer and the quantity ordered. This remarkable collection has been described by Mrs Sally Bird, of the Record Office, in *The Davison Collection in the Northumberland Record Office* (working paper no. PH 41/February 1985 of the History of the Book Trade in the North).

19. Thomas Hugo, *Bewick's Woodcuts: Impressions of upwards of two thousand Wood-blocks, engraved for the most part by Thomas & John Bewick* (London, 1870), p. 9.

20. Ref. LO42/D1368.

21. George Skelly, *Life of Thomas Bewick* (Alnwick, 1888), p. 15.

22. The figure of £500 given by Skelly is substantially more than Mr Iain Bain has found any record of in the Bewick ledgers and daybooks.

23. Skelly, *Bewick*, p. 21, writes 'The first portion of this catalogue would appear to have been printed about the year 1818, and the remaining portion shortly afterwards.

24. I have a bill, dated 21 September [1840], from Davison to John Procter, the Hartlepool printer, for various almanacs and chapbooks, and mentioning various cuts including 'a Tea Cut and a Cathedral Cut' (cf. nos. 57–88, 925–938, and 1030–1039, and 314, duplicated at 833).

25. p. 112, item 298.

26. Cf. W. A. Chatto and John Jackson, *A Treatise on Wood Engraving*, new edition (London, 1861), pp. 636–7. For a full description of the process see T. C. Hansard, *Typographia* (London, 1825), pp. 815–87. In the early 1960s, when I was preparing my paper for the Bibliographical Society, Mr John Whinham, of Alnwick, very kindly lent me two manuscript notebooks prepared by George Skelly and entitled 'Books printed at Alnwick'. On p. 11 of vol. ii is the transcription of a 'Catalogue of an Extensive and Valuable Stock of Books, Stationery, Woodcuts, Copper Plates, Stereotype Plates and Bookbinding and Printing Materials, which will be sold by auction . . . This stock the property of the late Mr. William Davison, Publisher, Alnwick, comprises above five tons of type and Stereotype Remainders, . . . the Stereotype Plates of several Children's Books &c, Stereo Ornaments, Mounted and unmounted, The Stereotype Foundry Plant . . .'

27. Presumably this was Mark Smith, John Catnach's former apprentice; he (or his firm) was actively printing in Alnwick until at least 1876.

28. The note at the foot of the invoice to John Procter, already mentioned, suggests that Davison was carrying out stereotyping for other printers from their own cuts. Perhaps he kept casts for himself by arrangement. This would help to explain his very large stock.

29. Letter in the collection of Mrs John Hack.

30. Burman, *An Account . . . 1781 to 1815*, p. 71.

31. In the collection of Dr John Johnson, Alnwick.

32. Letter in the collection of Iain Bain.

33. The first edition was Catnach's of 1805.

34. In the Burman Alnwick Collection in the University Library, Newcastle upon Tyne, there is not only a copy of this edition, but also of the earlier edition that Wilkie has simply divided up for the several characters to speak.

35. This book bears the name of Longmans in the imprint. Reference to the Longmans Commission Registers (by courtesy of the late Cyprian Blagden and Mrs B. M. Hurst) shows that, of eighteen copies sent to London by Davison on 24 October 1829, ten were deposited at Stationers' Hall and one at the Medical Depository; only seven were sold to yield a gross return to Davison of 2s. 3d.

36. Manuscript notebooks, vol. i, p. 63; see note 26 above.

37. Also the author of *An Essay towards a History of Hexham* (demy 8°, 1823).

38. The grangerized copy of C. C. Burman, *An Account of the Art of Typography as Practised in Alnwick from 1781 to 1815*, Alnwick, 1896, was very kindly given to me in the early 1960s by Mr Joseph Burman of Vancouver, Dr C. C. Burman's son.

39. Davison's *History*, 1822, pp. 232–6.

40. Manuscript notebooks, vol. i, pp. 135–7.

41. The title-page, which is found loose with the parts of this little work, is a bogus later production; the types used in the title are from much later in the century.

42. No. 11 of the part issue of de Buffon's *Natural History* carries an advertisement, dated July 1813, for the Bible ('Speedily will be published').

43. Manuscript notebooks, vol. i, p. 51.

44. Burman, *An Account*, pp. 62–3. The remainders are advertised in the *Alnwick Mercury* for 1 January 1857, in sheets at 25s. 'carefully collated ready for any bookbinder'.

45. Vol. i, p. 54.

46. *Bewick*, p. 16.

47. See, for example, introduction to Frances M. Thomson, *Newcastle Chapbooks in the Newcastle upon Tyne University Library*, Oriel Press, 1969.

48. The publisher's bound set of the *Mercury* from the first number to that for 1 March 1859 is part of the collection of Alnwick printing presented by Mr Joseph Burman, of Vancouver, to the former Alnwick Urban District Council, and placed by that body on permanent loan in the University Library, Newcastle upon Tyne. F. W. D. Manders, in his *Bibliography of British Newspapers: Durham and Northumberland* indicates that there is also a set of these early numbers in the British Library at Colindale.

49. *An Account*, pp. 357–8.

50. *Alnwick*, p. 14.

51. For an account of these printers' trains see *Printer's Trains*, Wylam, Allenholme Press, 1969.

52. A four-page list, dated 1826, of his engraved views and scriptural prints is to be found at the end of some copies of the 1826 poll-book of Northumberland, put out by Davison.

53. Catalogue title transcribed by Skelly (manuscript notebooks, vol. ii, pp. 11–13).

54. See, for example, advertisement in the *Alnwick Mercury* for 1 March 1858. The John Johnson Collection in the Bodleian Library has a splendid collection of these sheets from all parts of the country.

55. I have given a full list of these in my *Some Alnwick Caricatures*, Wylam, Allenholme Press, 1965.

56. *History of Alnwick*, 2nd edn., 1822, p. 222.

57. The same, pp. 223–9.

58. See, for example, the Annual reports of the Dispensary for 1824 and 1825.

59. See British Library 10352.cc.33 for the ballot paper, on which he is shown as chemist.

60. *James Catnach*, p. 18.

61. See, for example, a memorial, dated 7 November 1850, to the Board of the York, Newcastle, and Berwick Railway, seeking a reduction in the freight charge for coal (Alnwick UDC Collection).

62. 'An account . . .', p. 357.

CHECKLIST OF BOOKS PRINTED BY DAVISON

NOTES

1. The list includes, generally, only those publications with forty-eight pages or more.

2. A chronological list is not possible; too many of Davison's books are undated.

3. Works not handled by the author are proceeded by (*). These come from Burman's list (CCB), from Hugo (*The Bewick Collector*, 1866, and *Supplement*, 1868 – Hugo's catalogue number is given), or from advertisements in Davison's own publications. To assist identification locations of copies handled by (or, in a very few cases, reported to) the author are shown as follows:

AC	Alnwick Castle
BL	British Library
NCL	Central Library, Newcastle upon Tyne
ULN	University Library, Newcastle upon Tyne
Harding	the late Mr W. N. H. Harding of Chicago
Isaac	The author
Roscoe	the late Mr S. Roscoe of Harrow

4. In attempting to give the appropriate format due allowance has been made for trimming. The paper sizes used are, for the most part, taken from Johnson's *Typographia, or the Printers' Instructor*, London, 1824 (i, 610). The page size of the largest copy seen is also given to the nearest 0·1 in.

5. A simplified pagination is given. Where any of the prelims are paginated in roman numerals, the prelim pages are shown as though they had all been so paginated. Where there are too many prelims to fit in a consecutive run in this way, the excess is shown as a single figure before the roman numerals. Un-numbered pages are attached to their appropriate sequence (roman or arabic) without any indication that the page numbers have been assumed. This is true even at the end of a book, so long as the pages continue the text of the book; where they do not (e.g. where an advertisement is included) the page numbers assumed are shown in [square brackets]. The pagination of section titles is usually assumed in the arabic sequence. Where no prelim pages carry roman numerals, page numbers are assumed in the main arabic sequence.

6. Since one of the main interests of Davison's printing lies in the wood-engraving by Bewick and his workshop, the total number of illustrations is given where applicable. The following abbreviations are used:

f'p.	frontispiece, normally occupying a full page facing the title-page
f.o.p.	folding-out plate
vig.	vignette, i.e. an illustration occupying less than a full page
pl.	plate, i.e. an illustration given a full page to itself
orn.	ornament, i.e. a printer's flower, or a metallic or cast ornament (difficult to separate from vig., since Davison is said to have stereotyped all his illustrative material)
f.o.	folding out
t-p.	title-page
cold.	coloured
eng.	engraved

1. Adams, Thomas. The Poetical Works of Thomas Adams, Warkworth: consisting of the Battle of Trafalgar, and some miscellaneous pieces. Alnwick: Printed by and for W. Davison. 1811.
Fcp. 8° (in 4s) – 6·9 × 4·1 in. Pp. i–xii, 13–208. 15 vig. (Hugo 266) AC, BL, NCL, ULN, Isaac

2. Allan, James. The Life of James Allan, the celebrated Northumberland piper, and other branches of his extraordinary family. . . . A new edition, improved. Blyth: Printed and published by W. Guthrie . . . 1818.
Crown 8° (in 4s) – 8·2 × 5·2 in. Pp. 2, 1–384. F'p. + 3 pl. + 2 2-pp. music insets. On p. 384 imprint: 'Alnwick: Printed by W. Davison.' BL, NCL, ULN

3. Alnwick. The History of Alnwick, the County Town of Northumberland. Alnwick: Printed by and for W. Davison. 1812.
Demy 12° (in 6s) – 7·2 × 4·1 in. Pp. 1–142. F'p. + 1 vig. AC, Isaac

4. Alnwick. The History of Alnwick, the County Town of Northumberland. Alnwick: Printed by and for W. Davison. 1813.
Demy 12° (in 6s) – 7·2 × 4·1 in. Pp. 1–142. F'p. + 1 vig. (Hugo 277/4255) BL, NCL, ULN, Isaac

5. Alnwick. Description of Alnwick and Warkworth Castles, Alnwick and Huln Abbeys, and Warkworth Hermitage, with the poem of the Hermit of Warkworth. Alnwick: Printed by and for W. Davison. 1818.
Medium 18° (in 6s) – 5·8 × 3·5 in. Pp. 1–89, [90]. 4 pl. + 11 vig. ULN

*6. Alnwick. Description of Alnwick and Warkworth Castles, Alnwick and Huln Abbeys, and Warkworth Hermitage.
12°. Pp. 48. Woodcuts. (CCB) (This is possibly the first 48 pages of the item immediately above. These carry Davison's imprint at the foot of p. 48.)

7. Alnwick. A Descriptive and Historical View of Alnwick, the County Town of Northumberland; and of Alnwick Castle, Alnwick and Hulne Abbeys, Brislee Tower, the Borough of Alnwick, &c. Second edition, with numerous views, plans, and illustrations. Alnwick: Printed and published by W. Davison. MDCCCXXII.
Demy 8° (in 4s) – 8·9 × 5·5 in. Pp. 4, 9–334. F'p. (f.o.) + 7 f.o.p. + 12 pl. + 1 vig. (Hugo 440) (Also published in four parts in printed paper covers.) AC, BL, NCL, ULN, Isaac (also copy in parts)

8. Alnwick. Description of Alnwick Castle, and of Alnwick Abbey, Hulne Abbey, Brislee Tower, Warkworth Castle, and Warkworth Hermitage. A new edition, considerably enlarged and improved. To which is added, the Hermit of Warkworth, By Dr Percy, Bishop of Dromore. Alnwick: Printed and published by W. Davison, Bondgate Street. [1823]
Demy 18° (in 6s) – 5·9 × 3·6 in. Pp. 1–134. F'p. Date with imprint on p. 134. (Hugo 3818) NCL, ULN, Isaac

9. Alnwick. A Description of Alnwick Castle, Northumberland. For the use of visitors. Alnwick: W. Davison, Bondgate Street. MDCCCXLVI.
Demy 12° (in 6s) – 7·2 × 4·3 in. Pp. 3–40. 6 vig. (Some copies have a fold-out frontispiece.) BL

10. Alnwick. A Description of Alnwick Castle. For the use of visitors. Alnwick: Published by W. Davison, Bondgate Street. 1851.
Demy 12° (in 6s) – 7·4 × 4·6 in. Pp. 3–40. 6 vig. (Hugo 4400) NCL, ULN, Isaac

11. Alnwick Vocal Miscellany: a selection of the most esteemed songs, which possess any claim to poetical excellence, good sentiment, or humour. Alnwick: Printed and sold by W. Davison. 1816.
?Demy 12° (in 6s) – 6·6 × 4·0 in. Pp. 1–36. 1 vig. + 1 orn. ULN

12. Anderson, Robert. Ballads, in the Cumberland Dialect, by Robert Anderson. With notes, descriptive of the manners and customs of the Cumberland peasantry; a glossary of local words; and a life of the author. Alnwick: Printed by W. Davison, Bondgate Street. Sold by all booksellers.
Royal 32° (in 8s) – 4·9 × 3·0 in. Pp. i–xvi, 17–224. F'p. + 1 vig. + 11 orn. (Hugo 278/4258) BL, ULN, Isaac

13. Barrie, Alexander. A Collection of English prose and verse, for the use of schools, selected from different authors. To which are preferred, a few short lessons for beginners, with an exercise on spelling. . . . Also, an appendix, containing the principles of English grammar. . . . A new and correct edition. Alnwick: Printed and published by W. Davison. 1842.
Demy 12° – 7·1 × 4·3 in. Pp. 1–288. Isaac

14. Beattie, James. The Minstrel; or, the Progress of Genius: in two parts. With some other poems. By James Beattie, LL.D. With designs by Mr Thurston: and engraved on wood by Mr Clennel. Alnwick: Printed by Catnach and Davison. Sold by the booksellers in England and Scotland. 1807.
Fcp. 8° (in 4s) – 6·7 × 4·2 in. Pp. 1–142. 6 pl + 10 vig. BL, NCL, ULN, Isaac

15. Beattie, James. The Minstrel; or, the Progress of Genius: in two parts. With some other poems. . . . With designs by Mr Thurston: and engraved on wood by Mr Clennel. Alnwick: Printed by Catnach and Davison. Sold by the booksellers in England and Scotland. 1807.
Super-royal 8° (in 4s) – 9·7 × 6·8 in. Pp. 1–142. 6 pl. + 10 vig. '8s. in boards.' (Hugo 223) AC, BL, ULN, Isaac

16. Beattie, James. The Minstrel; or, the Progress of Genius: in two parts. With some other poems. . . . With designs by Mr Thurston: and engraved on wood by Mr Clennel. Alnwick: Printed by Catnach and Davison. Sold by the booksellers in England, Scotland, and Ireland. 1808.
Royal 8° (in 6s) – 7·0 × 4·2 in. '5s. in boards.' Pp. 1–142. 6 pl. + 10 vig. BL, NCL, ULN, Isaac

17. Beattie, James. The Minstrel; or, the Progress of Genius: in two parts. With some other poems. . . . With designs by Mr Thurston: and engraved on wood by Mr Clennel. Alnwick: Printed by W. Davison. Sold by the booksellers in England and Scotland. 1810.
Demy 12° (in 6s) – 7·1 × 4·2 in. '5s. in boards.' Pp. i–viii, 9–144. 6 pl. + 10 vig. BL, NCL, ULN, Isaac

18. Beattie, James. The Minstrel; or, the Progress of Genius: in two parts. With some other poems by James Beattie, LL.D. with his Life. Engravings on wood by Clennel from designs by Thurston. Alnwick: Printed by W. Davison.

Fcp. 8° – 6·3 × 3·8 in. Pp. i–vi, ix–xxvi, 27–198. (Contents may be at pp. v–vi or after p. 198.) Eng. f'p. + eng. t-p. + 6 pl. + 10 vig. NCL, ULN, Isaac

19. Bible. The universal Holy Bible; or complete Library of divine Knowledge; containing the Sacred Text . . . with marginal references. Illustrated with notes and annotations, critical and explanatory. . . . Embellished with superior engravings from paintings by the most celebrated artists ancient and modern. Vol. I [II]. Alnwick: Printed by and for W. Davison. [1820] [The above titles are engraved; there is also a letterpress title for the new testament and this is dated 1820.]
Demy f° – 16·8 × 10·5 in. Pages unnumbered. Collation: π² A–9R² 9S¹; π² A1 B–4S², A†–2L†², χ1 5A–8L². Eng. f'p. + eng. t-p. + 21 pl.; Eng. map + eng. t-p. + 26 pl. ULN, Isaac
(In part issue no. 11 of Buffon's *Natural History*, dated July 1813, in ULN, there is an advert. for the Bible 'speedily will be published'.)

20. Blair, Robert. The Grave, a Poem. By Robert Blair. To which is added Gray's Elegy in a country churchyard. With notes moral, and explanatory. The house appointed for all living. Job. Alnwick: Printed by Catnach and Davison. Sold by the booksellers in England, Scotland, and Ireland. 1808.
?Post 12° (in 6s) – 5·1 × 3·4 in. (severely cropped). Pp. xiv, 15–72. Eng. f'p. + 1 vig. + 2 orn. (Hugo 4206) Isaac

*21. Blair, Robert. The Grave, a Poem. By Robert Blair. To which is added Gray's Elegy. Alnwick: Printed by W. Davison. 1808.
12°. (Hugo 231)

22. Blair, Robert. The Grave, a poem. By Robert Blair. To which is added Gray's Elegy in a country churchyard. The house appointed for all living. Job. Alnwick: Printed by and for W. Davison, and sold by A. K. Newman & Co. London, J. and J. Robertson, & Oliver & Boyd Edinburgh. 1811.
Crown 18° (in 6s) – 5·4 × 3·5 in. Pp. 2, i–xii, 13–46. F'p. + 2 vig. (Hugo 4233) ULN

23. Blair, Robert. The Grave, a poem. By Robert Blair. To which is added Gray's Elegy written in a country church-yard. The house appointed for all living. Job. Alnwick: Printed and sold wholesale and retail by W. Davison.
Crown 18° (in 6s) – 5·5 × 3·5 in. Pp. i–xii, 13–47 [48]. F'p. + 1 orn. Isaac

24. Bow, W. F. Notions of the Nature of Fever, and of Nervous Action. . . . London: Printed for Longman, Rees, Orme, Browne, and Green; D. Lizars, Edinburgh; W. Davison, Alnwick; and E. Charnley. 1829.
Demy 8° (in 4s) – 9·0 × 5·6 in. Pp. i–iv, 1–100. BL, ULN

25. Brady, N. and Tate, N. A new version of the Psalms of David, fitted to the Tunes used in churches. . . . Compared with different editions, and carefully corrected. Alnwick: Printed by W. Davison. 1817.
Demy 8° (in 4s) – 8·3 × 5·2 in. [Pp. unnumbered] Collation: [ ]² B–C² D–P⁴ Q². Isaac

*26. British Reading Easy. 6d., 3d., and 1d. (From advertisement on back cover of 'Tom Thumb's Play Book'.)

27. Brown, W. H. Journal of a Voyage from London to Barbadoes. By William Henry Brown, Late of St Peter's, Leguan,

Demerara. To which are annexed a few poems by the same. Alnwick: Printed by W. Davison, Bondgate Street. To be had of the booksellers. 1836.
Fcp. 8° (in 4s) – 6·4 × 4·0 in. Pp. i–viii, 1–93 [94]. F'p. ULN, Isaac

*28. Burns, Robert. Poetical Works. In numbers. No. I. Catnach and Davison. [1807.]
Fcp. 8° (Advertisement in Beattie's *Minstrel*, 1807) (CCB)

29. Burns, Robert. The Poetical Works of Robert Burns; with his life. Ornamented with engravings on wood by Mr Bewick, from original designs by Mr Thurston. In two volumes. . . . Alnwick: Printed by Catnach and Davison. Sold by the booksellers in England, Scotland, and Ireland. 1808.
Fcp. 8° (in 4s) – 6·7 × 4·1 in. Pp. i–viii, 17–276 (p. iv misnumbered v); i–viii, 2, 9–266. 9 pl. + 23 vig.; 5 pl. + 17 vig. (sometimes with woodcut f'p. in vol. ii). (At end of glossary on p. 266 'Alnwick:—Printed by Catnach and Davison, 1808.') AC, NCL, ULN, Isaac, Roscoe

30. Burns, Robert. The Poetical Works of Robert Burns; with his life. Ornamented with engravings on wood by Mr Bewick, from original designs by Mr Thurston. In two volumes. Vol. I [II]. Alnwick: Printed by William Davison. Sold by the booksellers in England, Scotland and Ireland. 1808.
Fcp. 8° (in 4s) – 6·9 × 4·1 in. Pp. i–xlii, 43–266 (pp. 265–8 misnumbered 263–6 – also p. vi misnumbered 6). The notes for Vol. II (pp. 241–4) were printed as part of signature EE of Vol. I); i–viii (pp. v misnumbered vii, and viii misnumbered ix), 9–270. F'p. + 9 pl. + 25 vig. (in at least one copy there is a wood-engraved portrait of Burns facing p. xi; this is transposed from the frontispiece. This same copy has eng. f'p. and t-p. to both volumes in addition to the letterpress t-p.); 5 pl. + 22 vig. (At end of glossary on p. 270 'Anwick: Printed by W. Davison.') ULN, Isaac, Roscoe

31. Burns, Robert. The Poetical Works of Robert Burns. With his life. Engravings on wood by Bewick from designs by Thurston. Vol. I [II]. Alnwick: Printed by W. Davison. [1811.]
Fcp. 8° (in 4s) – 6·7 × 4·1 in. Pp. 4, i–xlii, 43–297 [298], 1–26 [in some copies this 26 p. glossary is at the end of vol. 2]; i–xii, 2, 13–320. Each vol. usually has eng. f'p. and t-p.; 9 pl. + 31 vig.; 9 pl. + 24 vig. (At end of glossary on p. 26 'Alnwick: Printed by W. Davison.' – following the glossary and probably conjugate with it is an advertisement for Fergusson's *Poetical Works* 'To Correspond with this edition of Burns Poems', dated 1811. This is also rarely found in printed boards dated 1812. This edition was also issued in parts, the covers of which in the single part (no. 10 – pp. 161–208 of vol. II) in ULN are dated 1815.) (Hugo 230) ULN, Isaac, Roscoe

*32. Burns, Robert. Works. With his life. New edition, with additions. 3 vols. (in 18 numbers). [1811]
(Advertisement in Blair's *Grave*, 1811. D. C. Thomson in *Life and Times of Bewick*, p. 218, says that the project was abandoned.) (CCB)

*33. Burns, Robert. Poetical Works. With his life. Engravings on wood from designs by Thurston. Vol. iv only.
Post 8°. Pp. xxiv + 359. (Not dated, but watermark in paper 1808 and 1814. The only four-volume edition of Burns, printed at Alnwick.) (CCB)

34. Burns, Robert. The Poems and Songs of Robert Burns. With a life of the author, and a glossary. Alnwick: Printed and published by W. Davison. 1828.
Fcp. 12° – 5·5 × 3·0 in. Pp. 2, i–viii, 9–336. F'p. + 20 vig. (The f'p. is tipped in and varies from one copy to another.) (Hugo 480) BL, ULN, Isaac

35. Burns, Robert. The Poems and Songs of Robert Burns. With a life of the author, and a glossary. Alnwick: Printed and published by W. Davison, and sold by J. Banks, Keswick.
Fcp. 12° – 5·5 × 3·0 in. Pp. 2, i–viii, 9–336. F'p. + 20 vig. (Except for the t-p., which appears to be conjugate with pp. vii–viii of the prelims, this is identical with the issue with the t-p. dated 1828.) ULN

36. A Cabinet of Natural History, containing pretty pictures of birds, animals, fishes, reptiles, serpents & insects. Embellished with engravings on wood, by Thomas Bewick of Newcastle. Alnwick: Printed at the Apollo Press, by and for W. Davison. 1809 [?1819]
This is no more than an alternative title-page (to be tipped in and displaying typography of a late nineteenth-century character) for *Natural History of British Quadrupeds* . . . ULN, Isaac

37. A Collection of Newspaper Extracts; being, with a few exceptions, taken from the newspapers of the day, and designed to afford some amusement to those who are fond of an every-day book. Alnwick: Printed by W. Davison, 22, Bondgate. MDCCCXXXIII.
Demy 12° (in 6s) – 7·3 × 4·3 in. Pp. i–viii, 1–220. 22 vig. + 2 orn. NCL, ULN

38. A Collection of Newspaper Extracts; being, with a few exceptions, taken from the newspapers of the day, and designed to afford some amusement to those who are fond of an every-day book. Alnwick: Printed by W. Davison, 22, Bondgate. MDCCCXXXIX.
Demy 12° (in 6s) – 7·0 × 4·3 in. Pp. i–viii, 1–220, vig. + 2 orn. NCL

39. A Collection of Newspaper Extracts; being, with a few exceptions, taken from the newspapers of the day, and designed to afford some amusement to those who are fond of an every-day book. Alnwick: Printed by W. Davison, 22, Bondgate. MDCCCXLII.
Demy 12° (in 6s) – 7·1 × 4·3 in. Pp. i–viii, 1–220. 22 vig. + 2 orn. (Hugo 503) NCL, ULN [There are a number of minor differences among these 'editions' which seem to demonstrate at least three forms of many signatures, but these are not always consistent to one 'edition'.]

40. Common Prayer, The Book of, and Administration of the Sacraments, and other rites and ceremonies of the Church, according to the use of the United Church of England and Ireland: together with the Psalter, or the Psalms of David, printed as they are to be said or sung in churches. Also, the companion to the altar, and the articles of religion. With notes critical and explanatory. Alnwick: Printed by W. Davison. 1817.
Demy 8° (in 4s, prelims in 2s) – 8·3 × 5·2 in. [Pp. unnumbered] Collation: [ ]² b–g² A–4F⁴ 4G–4I². F'p. + 4 pl. Isaac

41. Complete Ready Reckoner, enlarged and improved, containing tables ready cast up, showing the value of goods, &c.

from one-quarter to fifty-thousand with tables of interest, commission, the Imperial standard weights and measures, and other useful information.
Roy. 32°, bound 1s. 6d. (From advertisement on back cover of 'Tom Thumb's Play Book'.)

*42. Cooke's Universal Letter-Writer. 2s. 6d.
(From advertisement on inside cover of Ramsay's *Gentle Shepherd*, 1836.)

43. [Cottin, Sophie] Elizabeth; or, the Exiles of Siberia. A tale founded upon facts. Alnwick: Printed and published by W. Davison. 1821.
?Post 12° (in 6s) – 5·9 × 3·5 in. Pp. 113. (The advertisement on the back cover of this little booklet for nineteen titles, only six of which are in this checklist, suggests that the 'ghosts' in this list may have been 'published' by Davison, but not printed by him.) Isaac

44. Crozer, James. The Alnwick Unitarian Debate: second edition. To which are added an original allegory, and a review of Hyndman's Unitarian lectures, with introductory remarks in refutation of sceptical notions respecting the universal deluge, &c. By James Crozer, cousin to the late Capt. Cook, the circumnavigator. Alnwick: Printed and published by W. Davison, for the author. Sold also by J. Finlay, Mosley Street, Newcastle; P. Blair, Morpeth; J. Reid, Berwick; Henderson, Belford; Macdonald, Wooler; and all other booksellers. 1826.
Demy 12° (in 6s) – 7·4 × 4·3 in. Pp. 4, 1–244. NCL, ULN

45. [Davison, William] New Specimen of cast-metal ornaments and wood types, sold by W. Davison, Alnwick. n.d. [after 1837]
Demy 4° – 10·9 × 8·5 in. 130 leaves, printed one side only, unpaginated and unsigned. Contains 1082 impressions of Bewick wood-engravings, stock cuts, metal ornaments, wood letters, ornamental borders, etc., numbered and priced. Sometimes found without title-page. (Hugo 298) NCL, ULN, Isaac – This is the volume here reprinted

46. A Description of above three hundred Animals; or, an interesting natural history of quadrupeds, birds, fishes, serpents, and insects. Carefully abridged from Buffon, Swammerdam, Brookes, Goldsmith, &c. with upwards of 300 elegant engravings on wood. Alnwick: Printed by and for W. Davison. Sold by Longman, Hurst, Rees, Orme, and Brown, London, and all other booksellers. [1819]
Fcp. 12° (in 6s) – 5·5 × 3·4 in. Pp. i–iv, 5–324. 309 vig. The preface is dated 'May 14th, 1819'. In some places this is identical with *Natural History of British Quadrupeds* . . . (Hugo 415) ULN

47. Dickson, William. The Annual Address to the Berwickshire Naturalists' Club, delivered at the Anniversary Meeting, held at Alnmouth, in Northumberland, on Thursday, the 24th day of September, 1857 . . . Alnwick: Printed at the Mercury Office by William Davison. 1857.
Demy 8° – 8·4 × 5·3 in. Pp. 1–52. AC

48. Dickson, William. Communications by William Dickson, F.S.A. to the Berwickshire Naturalists' Club in the years 1857–58. Extracted from the Proceedings of the Club. Alnwick: Printed at the Mercury Office, by Wm. Davison, 22, Bondgate Street. 1858.
Demy 8° – 7·9 × 5·3 in. Pp. 1–16. NCL

49. Donaldson, Thomas. Poems, chiefly in the Scotish [thus] Dialect; both humourous [thus] and entertaining. By Thomas Donaldson, Weaver, Glanton. Entered at Stationers' Hall. Alnwick: Printed at the Apollo Press, by and for Wm. Davison, and sold by all other booksellers. 1809.
Demy 12° (in 6s) – 7·4×4·5 in. Pp. 2, i–xii, 13–225 [226], 227–34. (A dedication to the Duke of Northumberland is tipped in between pp. ii and iii – pp. 227–34 list of subscribers) 33 vig. (Hugo 244) AC, BL, NCL, ULN, Isaac

*50. Ferguson, James. A key to Hutton's Arithmetic. 1842.
8°. Pp. vi, 281. (CCB)

51. Fergusson, Robert. The Poetical Works of Robert Ferguson [thus] with his life. Engravings on wood by Bewick. Vol. I [II]. Alnwick: Printed by W. Davison. [1811]
Fcp. 8° (in 4s) – 6·7×4·1 in. Pp. i–viii, 9–273 [274]; i–viii, 9–254 (with 2 pp. Adverts at end). Each vol. has eng. f'p. and t-p.; 6 pl.+26 vig.; 6 pl.+23 vig. (Hugo 305) AC, BL, NCL, ULN, Isaac

52. Gay, John. Fables, by John Gay. With upwards of one hundred embellishments. Alnwick: Printed by W. Davison, Bondgate Street. 1842.
Demy 12° (in 6s) – 7·4×4·4 in. Pp. i–xii, 1–216. F'p.+115 vig. (Hugo 4383) BL, ULN, Isaac

*53. Geography for Children, with maps. 1s. 6d.
(From advertisement on inside front cover of Ramsay's *Gentle Shepherd*, 1836.)

54. Goldsmith, Oliver. The Poetical Works of Oliver Goldsmith. Hoc amet, hoc spernat promissi carminis auctor. Alnwick: Printed by W. Davison and sold by the Booksellers in England & Scotland. 1812.
Demy 18° (in 6s) – 5·8×3·6 in. Pp. i–viii, 9–74. F'p. (Hugo 271/5415) BL, NCL, ULN, Isaac

55. Goldsmith, Oliver. The Vicar of Wakefield, a tale; by Dr Goldsmith. Sperate miseri, cavete felices. Alnwick: Printed by W. Davison. Sold by booksellers in Great Britain. 1812.
Demy 12° (in 6s) – 7·4×4·5 in. Pp. 2, 1–216. F'p.+1 vig. BL, ULN

*56. Goldsmith, Oliver. Dr Goldsmith's Abridgement of the History of England. . . . A new edition. London. Printed for the Booksellers. Sold wholesale and retail by W. Davison, Bondgate Street, Alnwick. 1828.
Post 8°. Pp. 362. (Probably printed by Davison) (CCB)

57. Hindmarsh, [Isabella]. The Cave of Hoonga, a Tongaen Tradition, in two cantos. And other poems. By Miss Hindmarsh. Alnwick: Printed for the author by W. Davison. 1818.
Fcp. 8° (in 4s) – 6·7×4·1 in. Pp. i–xvi, 17–254. AC, BL, ULN, Isaac

*58. Housekeeper's Manual of Cookery and Domestic Economy, The. 1855.
(Advertisement in *Alnwick Mercury*, 1 Feb. 1855: 'Complete in four numbers at 1d. each.')

*59. Hutcheson, Revd A. The Apocalypse its own Interpreter: or, a guide to the study of the Book of Revelation. Second edition. 1834.
12°. Pp. viii, 316. (CCB)

60. Hutton, Charles. Davison's Edition. A Complete Treatise on Practical Arithmetic, and Book-keeping, both by single and double entry. Adapted to the use of schools. By Charles Hutton, LL.D., F.R.S., &c. A new edition, corrected and enlarged; comprising the Imperial standard weights and measures, with numerous additions and improvements. By James Ferguson, Teacher of the Mathematics, Borough School, Alnwick. Alnwick: Printed by and for W. Davison. 1828. [Price 2s. 6d. Bound. – Liberal allowance to Schools.]
Demy 12° (in 6s) – 7·0×4·2 in. Pp. i–viii, 1–232. BL

61. Hutton, Charles. Davison's Enlarged Stereotype Edition. A Complete Treatise on Practical Arithmetic, and Book-keeping, both by single and double entry. Adapted to the use of schools. By Charles Hutton, LL.D., F.R.S., &c. A new and correct edition, with numerous additions and improvements, comprising upwards of five hundred new questions, and Imperial standard weights and measures with the latest amendments. By James Ferguson, Teacher of Mathematics, Borough School, Alnwick. Alnwick: Published by W. Davison, Bondgate Street, and to be had of all booksellers. [Price 2s. 6d. Bound. – Liberal allowance to Schools.] [not before 1842]
Demy 12° – 7·1×4·2 in. Pp. i–vi, 7–256. (Preface dated 29 April 1835; but parcel bill on p. 127 dated 7 Nov. 1842.) Isaac

62. Hyndman, J. S. Lectures on the Principles of Unitarianism. By J. S. Hyndman, Minister of the Unitarian Chapel, Alnwick. . . . Alnwick: Printed and sold by W. Davison. Sold also by C. Fox & Co., D. Eaton, and R. Hunter. London, and by other booksellers. 1824.
Royal 18° (in 6s) – 6·6×4·0 in. Pp. i–vi, 9–142. BL

*63. [Hyndman, Revd J. S.] A Defence of Lectures on Unitarianism, in Reply to the Animadversions of the Revd William Procter, junior, M.A. 1825.
12°. Pp. 47. (CCB)

*64. Johnson's Dictionary, with an Account of the heathen deities, &c. Price 3s. bound. [1836]
(From advertisement on inside front cover of Ramsay's *Gentle Shepherd*, 1836.)

65. Le Clerc, G. L., Count de Buffon. The System of Natural History, written by M. de Buffon, carefully abridged: and the natural history of insects; compiled chiefly from Swammerdam, Brookes, Goldsmith, &c. embellished with elegant engravings on wood, in four volumes. Vol. I [II III IV]. Alnwick: Printed by and for W. Davison. 1814.
Fcp. 8° (in 4s) – 6·7×4·0 in. Pp. i–iv, iii–vi, 9–336; i–iv, 9–324; i–iv, 9–332; i–iv, 9–308. 63 vig.; 109 vig.; 117 vig.; 28 vig. (Hugo 283) This was earlier issued in parts. Part II, containing pp. 321–4 of vol. ii and pp. 9–68 of vol. iii, has an advert. for the *Universal Holy Bible* dated July 1813. BL, ULN, Isaac

66. Le Clerc, G. L., Count de Buffon, Oliver Goldsmith and others. A History of the Earth and animated Nature: from M. de Buffon, Goldsmith and others. Embelished [thus] with upwards of one hundred elegant copper-plates engraved on purpose representing some hundreds of figures. In two volumes. Vol. I [II] Alnwick: Printed at the Apollo Press, by and for W. Davison. And sold by all the booksellers in England and Scotland. 1810.
Demy 12° (in 6s) – 7·4×4·3 in. Pp. 2, i–viii, 13–278; 2, i–vi,

13–270 (wrongly numbered 272). F'p.+34 pl.+1 vig.; 1 f.o.p.+ 66 pl.+2 vig. (Hugo 5408) ULN, Isaac

67. Luckley, J. L. The Pleasures of Sight, and other poems. By John Lamb Luckley, Alnwick. . . . Alnwick: Printed for the author, by W. Davison, Bondgate Street. 1847.
Demy 12° (in 6s) – 7·3 × 4·3 in. Pp. 1–36. 2 vig. BL, NCL

68. Luckley, J. L. The Pleasures of Sight, and other poems. By John Lamb Luckley, Alnwick. Second edition, with additions. . . . Alnwick: Printed for the author, by W. Davison, Bondgate Street. 1847.
Demy 12° (in 6s) – 7·2 × 4·3 in. Pp. 1–48. 2 vig. NCL, ULN

69. Markham, William. An Introduction to Spelling and Reading English; . . . and a Treatise on the Arts of Writing and Arithmetic; also six familiar fables, Adorned with proper sculptures, to delight and instruct Youth. . . . Alnwick: Stereotyped and Printed by W. Davison. Sold by all Booksellers. n.d.
Demy 12° – 6·9 × 4·0 in. Pp. 1–144. F'p.+21 vig.+1 orn. 'Davison's Stereotype Edition.' (Hugo 494, ?495, ?4373) BL, Isaac [copy dated 1847]

70. Mavor, William. The English Spelling Book, accompanied by a progressive series of easy and familiar lessons, intended as an introduction to the reading and spelling of the English language. By William Mavor, LL.D. A new edition, corrected and improved. Alnwick: Stereotyped and printed by W. Davison, Bondgate Street. A liberal allowance to schools.
Demy 12° – 7·0 × 4·1 in. Pp. 1–168. F'p.+47 vig. NCL, ULN

*71. Modern Atlas, containing 26 coloured maps from the best authorities. Price 10s. 6d., half-bound. [1836]
4° (From advertisement on inside front cover of Ramsay's Gentle Shepherd, 1836.)

72. A Natural History of Birds, Quadrupeds, Fishes, Reptiles, Serpents, Butterflies and Insects, with 153 engravings on wood. By Thomas Bewick, of Newcastle-upon-Tyne. Alnwick. Printed at the Apolo [thus] Press, By and for W. Davison. 1819.
This is no more than a loose title-page. ULN

73. A Natural History of British Quadrupeds [Foreign Quadrupeds] [British Birds] [Water Birds] [Foreign Birds] [Fishes] [Reptiles, Serpents, and Insects]. Thirty-two [thirty-two] [thirty-two] [thirty-four] [thirty-two] [forty] [thirty-four] engravings on wood. Alnwick: Printed and sold wholesale and retail by W. Davison.
Fcp. 12° (in 6s) – 5·5 × 3·5 in. Pp. 1–36, 1–36, 1–36, 1–36, 1–36, 1–36, 1–36 (7 parts in all). F'p.+33+34+35+34+34+40+35 vig. (Hugo 284–97, 4263) NCL, ULN, Isaac
Some copies show watermarks of 1817 and 1819

74. A new English Spelling-book; or, an easy introduction to spelling and reading, containing a variety of familiar lessons, adapted to the capacity of youth. A new edition, enlarged and improved. Alnwick: Stereotyped and printed by W. Davison, 22, Bondgate Street; and sold by all booksellers.
Demy 18° (in 6s) – 5·5 × 3·5 in. Pp. i–iv, 5–144. 9 vig.+4 orn. ULN

75. The New Reading made easy; consisting of a variety of useful lessons. Alnwick: Published by W. Davison. Price twopence.
Demy 18° – 5·9 × 3·7 in. Pp. 2, 1–33, [34]. 37 vig. (Hugo 4402) ULN, Isaac

76. The Northumberland Poll-Book; containing a list of the freeholders who voted at the contested elections for the County of Northumberland in the years 1747–8, 1774, and in Feb. and March, 1826. Including a complete collection of the papers which appeared in 1774, and the authentic papers, speeches, &c. relating to the election in Feb. and March, 1826. Alnwick: Printed and published by W. Davison. 1826.
Demy 8° (in 4s) – 9·0 × 5·5 in. Pp. 2, 1–249 [250], 1–55 [56]. AC, BL, NCL, ULN, Isaac

77. The Northumbrian Minstrel: a choice selection of Songs. Alnwick: Printed by W. Davison. 1811. [Nos. I, II, & III]
Fcp 12° (in 6s) – 5·3 × 3·4 in. Pp. 1–48, 1–48, 1–48. F'p.+1 vig.; F'p.+1 vig.; F'p.+1 vig. Title-page to each part. AC, NCL, ULN

78. Percy, Thomas. The Hermit of Warkworth. A Northumberland Ballad in three fits. By Dr Thos Percy, Bishop of Dromore. With designs by Mr Craig: and engraved on wood by Mr Bewick. Second Edition. Alnwick: Printed and sold by J. Catnach. Sold by Wilson and Spence, York. 1807.
Crown 4° – 9·1 × 6·3 in. Pp. i–xiv, 15–182. 3 pl.+10 vig. Title-page and pp. 102 and 182 carry Catnach's imprint, but the grey-green printed board covers (in which it may be found) carry the imprint 'Printed by Catnach and Davison' (with the same date, 1807). Pp. 103–82 are not always bound with The Hermit; they contain descriptions of Warkworth Hermitage, Alnwick and Huln Abbeys, and of a ride in Huln Park. When these are included there is a half-title which gives all this information. The NCL copy contains both half-titles – on the shorter is '7s. 6d. in boards'. In ULN there is a copy with its original paper cover of pp. 103–82 with the title 'The Descriptions of Warkworth Hermitage, Alnwick, and Warkworth Castles, Alnwick, and Huln Abbeys, and a descriptive ride in Huln Park . . .'. Alnwick: Printed by Catnach and Davison. AC, NCL

79. Percy, Thomas. The Hermit of Warkworth. A Northumberland Tale. In three parts. By Dr Thos Percy, Bishop of Dromore. With descriptions of Warkworth Hermitage, Alnwick and Warkworth Castles, Alnwick and Hulne Abbeys, and a descriptive ride in Hulne Park. Alnwick: Printed and sold by W. Davison. Price 1s. 8d. in boards. 1808.
Crown 18° (in 6s) – 5⅜ × 3½ in. Pp. i–viii, 9–48, 101–82. F'p.+2 vig. Harding (who kindly prepared a description of this chapbook)

*80. Percy, Thomas. The Hermit of Warkworth: a Northumberland Tale. In three parts. Adorned with engravings by Mr Bewick. 1808.
12°. Pp. xii, 70. Published at 1s. 6d. (CCB)

*81. Percy, Thomas. The Hermit of Warkworth: a Northumberland Tale. In three parts. Adorned with engravings on wood by Mr Bewick. 1808.
18°. Pp. viii, 48. (CCB)

82. Percy, Thomas. The Hermit of Warkworth. A Northumberland Tale. In three parts. By Dr Thos Percy, Bishop of Dromore. Adorned with engravings on wood by Mr Bewick. Alnwick: Printed and sold by W. Davison. 1810.
Crown 18° (in 6s) – 5·1 × 3·2 in. Pp. i–xii, 13–72. F'p.+4 pl.+3 vig. Isaac

[35]

83. Percy, Thomas. The Hermit of Warkworth. A Northumberland Tale. By Dr Percy, Bishop of Dromore. Adorned with engravings on wood by Mr Bewick. Alnwick: Printed and sold by W. Davison. 1811.
Crown 18° (in 6s) – $5\frac{3}{8} \times 3\frac{5}{16}$ in. Pp. i–xii, 13–72. F'p.+7 pl.+2 vig. Harding (who kindly prepared a description of this chapbook)

84. Percy, Thomas. The Hermit of Warkworth. A Northumberland Tale. In three parts. By Dr Thos Percy, Bishop of Dromore. Adorned with engravings on wood by Mr Bewick. Alnwick: Printed by W. Davison, and sold by Oliver and Boyd, Edinburgh 1811
Crown 18° (in 6s) – $5\cdot2 \times 3\cdot3$ in. Pp. i–xii, 13–72. F'p.+7 pl.+3 vig. (Price 1s. 6d.) ULN

85. Percy, Thomas. The Hermit of Warkworth: a Northumberland Tale. In three parts. By Dr Thomas Percy, Bishop of Dromore. Adorned with engravings on wood by Mr Bewick. Alnwick: Printed and sold by W. Davison. 1818.
Crown 18° (in 6s) – $5\cdot3 \times 3\cdot4$ in. Pp. i–viii. 9–54. F'p.+3 pl.+1 vig. ULN

86. Percy, Thomas. The Hermit of Warkworth: a Northumberland tale. In three parts. By Dr T. Percy, Bishop of Dromore. With engravings on wood by Bewick. Alnwick: Printed and sold by W. Davison. 1821.
?Foolscap 12° (in 6s) – $5\cdot3 \times 3\cdot3$ in. Pp. viii, 9–50. 4 pl. (Hugo 4325) Isaac

*87. Percy, Thomas. The Hermit of Warkworth: [etc.] With engravings on wood by Bewick. 1825.
18°. Pp. viii, 50. (A reprint of 1821 edition) (Hugo 4345)

88. Percy, Thomas. The Hermit of Warkworth, a Northumberland Tale, in three fits. . . . Illustrated with engravings by Bewick, from designs by Craig. Alnwick: Printed by W. Davison, Bondgate Street. MDCCCXLI.
Post 8° (in 4s) – $7\cdot5 \times 4\cdot7$ in. Pp. i–xii, 13–88. F'p.+12 pl.+4 vig. (Hugo 4381) ULN (see note to Wilkie's *Hermit*), Isaac

89. Percy, Thomas. The Hermit of Warkworth, a Northumberland Tale. In three parts. By Dr Thomas Percy, Bishop of Dromore. With an account of Warkworth Hermitage and Warkworth Castle. Alnwick: W. Davison, 22, Bondgate Street. Sold by all booksellers. n.d. [after 1847]
Demy 18° (in 6s) – $5\cdot6 \times 3\cdot5$ in. Pp. i–vi, 7–72. F'p.+2 pl.+12 vig. (Hugo 308) BL, NCL, ULN, Isaac

90. The Poll-Book of the Contested Election for the County of Northumberland, from June 20th to July 6th, 1826. Including a complete collection of the Addresses and Speeches of the candidates, &c. and the authentic papers published by the different parties from the commencement of their canvass to the termination of the contest. Alnwick: Printed and published by W. Davison. 1827.
Demy 8° (in 4s) – $8\cdot8 \times 5\cdot5$ in. Pp. 2, 1–381 [382]. BL (part only), NCL, ULN, Isaac

91. The Poll-Book of the Contested Election for the Northern Division of the County of Northumberland, taken on the 10th and 11th days of August, 1847, at Alnwick, Belford, Berwick, Elsdon, Morpeth, and Wooler, including the Addresses, Speeches, &c. of the candidates. Alnwick: Printed and sold by W. Davison, 22, Bondgate Street. 1847.
Demy 8° (in 4s) – $9\cdot0 \times 5\cdot6$ in. Pp. 1–119 [120]. AC, BL, NCL, ULN, Isaac

*92. Pope, Alexander. Works. 8 vols. [1809]
24s. in boards. (Advertisement on cover of Donaldson's *Poems*.) (CCB)

*93. Probert, William [Editor]. Collection of hymns, from various authors; for the use of Ebenezer Chapel.
12°. Pp. 250. (CCB)

94. [Probert, William] The Gododin, and the Odes of the Months, translated from the Welsh . . . [1820] London: Sold by E. Williams, 11, Strand, Bookseller to the Prince Regent and to the Duke and Duchess of York; W. Davison, Alnwick; E. Charnley, Newcastle upon Tyne; and P. Blair, Morpeth.
Post 8° (in 4s) – $7\cdot4 \times 4\cdot6$ in. Pp. i–vi, 7–113 [114], 6 (6 pp. of subscribers' names at end). 1 vig. (Hugo 4321) BL, NCL

95. Ramsay, Allan. The Gentle Shepherd, a Scots Pastoral, in five acts. By Allan Ramsay. Alnwick: Printed and sold by W. Davison. 1830.
Post 12° (in 6s) – $6\frac{3}{8} \times 3\frac{3}{4}$ in. Pp. 1–60. F'p.+1 vig. (Hugo 4368) Harding (who kindly prepared a description of this chapbook)

96. Ramsay, Allan. The Gentle Shepherd, a Scots Pastoral, in five acts. By Allan Ramsay. Alnwick: Printed and sold by W. Davison. 1836.
Demy 18° (in 6s) – $5\cdot7 \times 3\cdot6$ in. Pp. 1–60. F'p.+1 vig. (Hugo 492–3) ULN, Isaac

*97. Reading made quite easy; or a new English primer of easy and progressive lessons. 1836 .
Price 6d., half bound. (From advertisement on inside front cover of Ramsay's *Gentle Shepherd*, 1836.) This is not the same as a 2d. chapbook 'The new Reading Made Easy; consisting of a variety of Useful Lessons. Alnwick: Published by W. Davison. Price twopence.'

98. The Repository of select Literature; being an elegant assemblage of curious, scarce, entertaining, and instructive pieces. In prose and verse. Adorned with beautiful engravings by Bewick, etc. Alnwick: Printed by W. Davison. Sold by the Booksellers in England and Scotland. 1808. [Vol. ii runs '. . . Bewick, &c. In two volumes. Vol. II . . . 1809']
Demy 18° (in 6s) – $5\cdot6 \times 3\cdot6$ in. Pp. 1–413 [414]; 1–385 [386]. 11 pl.+4 vig.+2 orn; 10 pl.+7 vig.+2 orn. (Hugo 232, 4204) ULN

99. Service, James. The Wandering Knight of Dunstanborough Castle, a Northumbrian legend: and miscellaneous poems. By James Service. Alnwick: Printed for the Author, by William Davison. MDCCCXXII.
Fcp. 8° (in 4s) – $6\cdot7 \times 4\cdot1$ in. Pp. 1–136. BL, NCL

100. Service, James. Metrical Legends of Northumberland: containing the traditions of Dunstanborough Castle, and other poetical romances. With notes and illustrations. . . . Alnwick: Printed and sold by W. Davison. To be had of all booksellers. 1834.
Demy 12° (in 6s) – $7\cdot5 \times 4\cdot4$ in. Pp. v–x, 11–160. 11 vig. (Hugo 489, 4372) AC, BL, NCL, ULN, Isaac

101. Sopwith, T. An Account of the Mining District of Alston Moor, Weardale, and Teesdale, in Cumberland and Durham; comprising descriptive sketches of the scenery, antiquities, geology, and mining operations, in the upper dales of the rivers Tyne, Wear, and Tees. By T. Sopwith, Land and Mine Surveyor. Alnwick: Printed by and for W. Davison. Sold also by the booksellers in Northumberland, Durham, Cumberland, &c. MDCCCXXXIII.
Demy 12° (in 6s) – 7·5 × 4·5 in. Pp. 2, i–viii, 1–184. Cold. f'p.+6 vig. On p. 184 advertisements. BL, NCL, ULN, Isaac

102. Sopwith, T. Description and Use of an Improved Levelling Stave. By T. Sopwith, F.G.S., Land and Mine Surveyor, Member of the Institution of Civil Engineers. Printed for the Author. n.d.
Post 8° – 6·9 × 4·3 in. Pp. 1–12, 4 (4 pp. advertisements). Carries Davison's imprint on p. 12. NCL

*103. Thompson, Thomas. A complete repository of Scottish Strathspeys, selected from the works of celebrated composers, by Thomas Thompson; interspersed with original compositions now printed for the first time. [1854]
Oblong demy 8°. Monthly parts (CCB) (This is advertised in the first issue of the *Alnwick Mercury*, June 1854. Numbers 1 and 2 were then ready and no. 3 would be ready on 1 August 1854. The cost of each number was 3d.)

104. A Treatise on Breeding, Rearing and Feeding Cheviot and Black-faced Sheep in High Districts. With some account of and a complete cure for that fatal malady the Rot; together with observations on laying out and conducting a store farm. By a Lammermuir Farmer. Second edition. Alnwick: Printed by W. Davison, Bondgate Street. 1827.
Demy 8° (in 4s) – 8·5 × 5·3 in. Pp. i–xliv, 1–196. (With errata slip.) NCL

105. The Tyneside Songster, a collection of comic and descriptive songs, chiefly in the Newcastle dialect. Alnwick: Printed and sold by W. Davison, Bondgate Street.
Demy 18° (in 6s) – 6·0 × 3·6 in. Pp. 4, i–iv, 5–144. F'p.+3 vig. (Hugo 460) AC, ULN, Isaac

106. The Tyneside Songster, a choice collection of comic, satirical, and descriptive songs, in the Newcastle dialect. Alnwick: Stereotyped and printed by W. Davison, 22, Bondgate Street. [Price one shilling.]
Demy 18° (in 6s) – 5·6 × 3·5 in. Pp. 1–108. 1 vig.+2 orn. ULN, Isaac

*107. Universal Measurer, for the use of builders, farmers, surveyors, mechanics, cattle dealers, &c., containing accurate tables with explanations and examples of superficial or flat measure, timber measure, cubic or solid measure and value of land, weight of cattle, &c. 2s. bound. (From advertisement on back cover of 'Tom Thumb's Play Book')

*108. Walker's Pronouncing Dictionary, new edition corrected, and enlarged with upwards of 3000 words, by the Revd John Davis, A.M. Price 9s. (From advertisement on inside front cover of Ramsay's *Gentle Shepherd*, 1836.)

109. Watts, Isaac. Hymns and spiritual Songs, in three books. . . . By I. Watts, D.D. . . . Alnwick: Printed by and for W. Davison. 1822.
Crown 16° (in 8s) – 5·0 × 3·6 in. Pp. i–iv, 5–320. ULN

110. Wilkie, Robert. The Hermit of Warkworth, as adapted for theatrical representation. By Robert Wilkie, Esq. Alnwick: Printed and sold by W. Davison, Bondgate Street. MDCCCXLI.
Crown 12° (in 6s) – 6·8 × 4·1 in. Pp. 1–60. F'p.+8 pl.+2 vig. (A copy of the 1841 edition of the *Hermit*, in the University Library, Newcastle upon Tyne, is inscribed by Wilkie to Miss B. Inverarity on 2 July 1841. Apparently in the same hand are a number of annotations dividing the text in the same way as in this theatrical version.) (Hugo 501) ULN, Isaac

111. Wright, A. B. An Essay towards a History of Hexham: in three parts . . . with descriptive sketches of the scenery and natural history of the neighbourhood . . . Alnwick: Printed and published by W. Davison. Sold also by the principal Booksellers in Hexham, Newcastle, Shields, Morpeth, Berwick, Durham, Carlisle, &c. 1823.
Demy 8° (in 4s) – 8·8 × 5·5 in. Pp. i–xii. 9–246. 1 f.o.p.+1 pl.+ 1 vig. AC, BL, NCL, ULN, Isaac

A NOTE ON METAL CASTS

It is not certain when duplicate casts in type metal of small ornaments and initials were first made. A method for making casts using sand or plaster was described in a handbook published by the Lübeck printer Samuel Struck in 1715 (*Neu-verfassetes auff der löbl. Kunst-Buchdruckerey nützlich zu gebrauchendes Format-Buch*, Leipzig and Lübeck). From the late eighteenth century, cast ornaments appear to have been commonly made using type-metal matrices obtained by a method that was first described in a work published in Erfurt by J. M. Funcke in 1740 (*Kurtze, doch nützliche Anleitung von Form- und Stahl-Schneiden*). The invention of the process is attributed to the Leipzig wood engraver Martin Seltsam or Selzam by C. G. Täubel in his *Wörterbuch der Buchdruckerkunst und Schriftgiesserey* (Vienna, 1805). Making casts in this manner came to be known in German as *abklatschen*, from which the French *clicher*, and hence *cliché*, is apparently derived. An alternative French word was *polytyper*. This was sometimes used in English, but *dabbing* was an expressive word used by English typefounders, although it is rarely seen in print.

The first known commercial specimen of cast ornaments was issued by William Caslon III in 1786 (misdated 1784 in the catalogue of the Sohmian collection at Stockholm, and in subsequent literature). Further specimens of cast ornaments were issued by Caslon III in 1795 and 1798, by Fry and Steele in 1793, 1794 and 1805, and cast ornaments are a prominent feature of the specimen of S. and C. Stephenson, 1796.

Typefounders' specimens of the nineteenth century from about 1820 commonly display a selection of cast ornaments at the back of the book, but there continued to be specialist makers of ornaments. The Parisian firm of Durouchail was one of them, with a folio specimen, *Épreuves des divers ormenens typographiques gravés sur bois et polytypés*, in 1828. Only one copy is known of two English specimen books issued in the 1820s, the twenty-three leaf *Specimen of stereotype ornaments* of the wood engraver Matthew Urlwin Sears (Islington, 1825), and the *Specimens of stereotype casting* of the typefounder L. I. or Louis Jean Pouchée (not dated, but probably between 1823 and 1830, when his foundry was sold). Both of these specimens show elaborate ornamented types, and the Pouchée specimen, a substantial quarto which has only recently come to light, is particularly interesting since it confirms the tentative attribution to Pouchée of the remarkable surviving set of decorated alphabets engraved on wood of which sample letters were shown in the Society's *Journal* no. 2 (1966), and it adds some previously unknown designs to these. (The complete alphabets are currently being printed from the original wood blocks, for publication in the near future.) A few of Pouchée's blocks appear in the Davison specimen now reproduced in facsimile.

JAMES MOSLEY

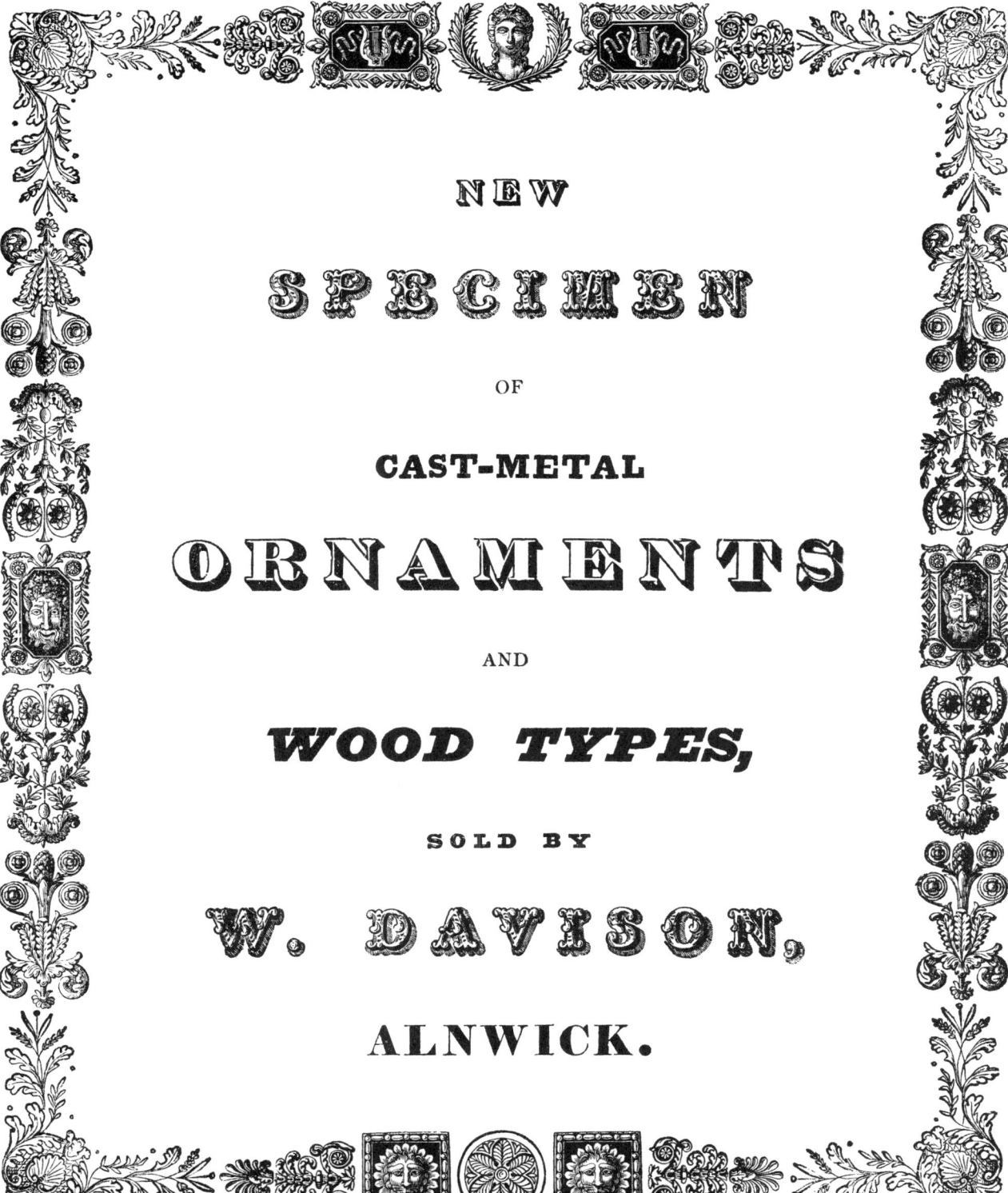

NEW

SPECIMEN

OF

CAST-METAL

ORNAMENTS

AND

WOOD TYPES,

SOLD BY

W. DAVISON,

ALNWICK.

No. 1,—10s. 6d.

No. 2,—10s. 6d.

No. 3,—10s. 6d.

No. 4,—10s. 6d.

No. 5,—10s 6d.

No. 6,—10s. 6d.

No. 7,—10s. 6d.

No. 8,—10s. 6d.

No. 9,—10s. 6d.

No. 10,—10s. 6d.

No. 11,—10s. 6d.

No. 12,—10s. 6d.

No. 13,—10s. 6d.

No. 14,—10s. 6d.

No. 15, —10s. 6d.

No. 16,—10s. 6d.

No. 17,—10s. 6d.

No. 18,—10s. 6d.

No. 19,—10s. 6d.

No. 20,—10s. 6d.

No. 21,—10s. 6d.

No. 22,—10s. 6d.

No. 23,—10s. 6d

No. 24,—10s. 6d.

No. 25,—10s. 6d.

No. 26.—10s. 6d.

No. 27, —10s. 6d.

No. 28,—10s. 6d.

No. 29.—10s. 6d.

No 30.—10s. 6d.

No. 31,—9s. 6d.

No. 32,—9s. 6d.

No. 33,—10s. 0d.

No. 34.—9s 6d.

No. 35,—10s. 6d.

No. 36,—7s. 6d.

No. 37,—10s. 6d.

No. 38,—10s. 6d.

No. 39,—15s.

No. 40,—10s. 6d.

No. 41,—10s. 6d.

No. 42,—10s. 6d.

No. 43,—10s 6d.

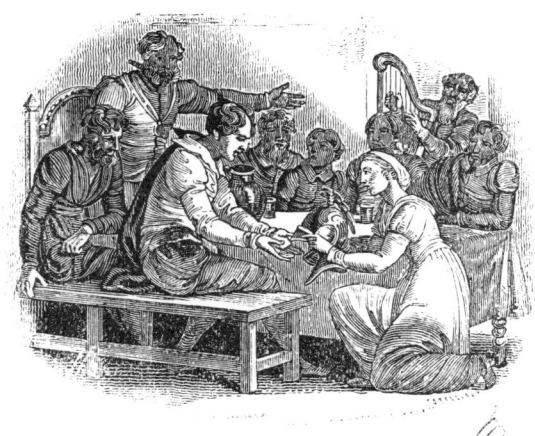 

No. 44,—15s.

No. 45,—10s. 6d.

No. 46,—10s. 6d.

No. 47,—15s.

No. 48,—3s. 6d.

No. 49,—3s. 6d.

No. 50,—15s.

No. 51,—12s.

No. 52,—12s.

No. 53,—12s.

No. 54,—12s.

No. 55,—12s.

No. 56,—12s.

No. 57,—8s.

No. 58,— 6s.

No. 59,—8s.

No. 60,—6s.

No 61,—8s.

No 62.—6s.

No. 63,—10s.

No. 64,—4s. 6d.

No. 65,—4s. 6d.

No. 66,—12s. 6d.

No. 67,—8s. 6d.

No. 68,—7s. 6d.

No. 69,—4s.

No. 70,—5s.

No. 71,—7s. 6d.

No. 72,—7s. 6d.

No. 73,—13s. 6d.

No. 74,—12s.

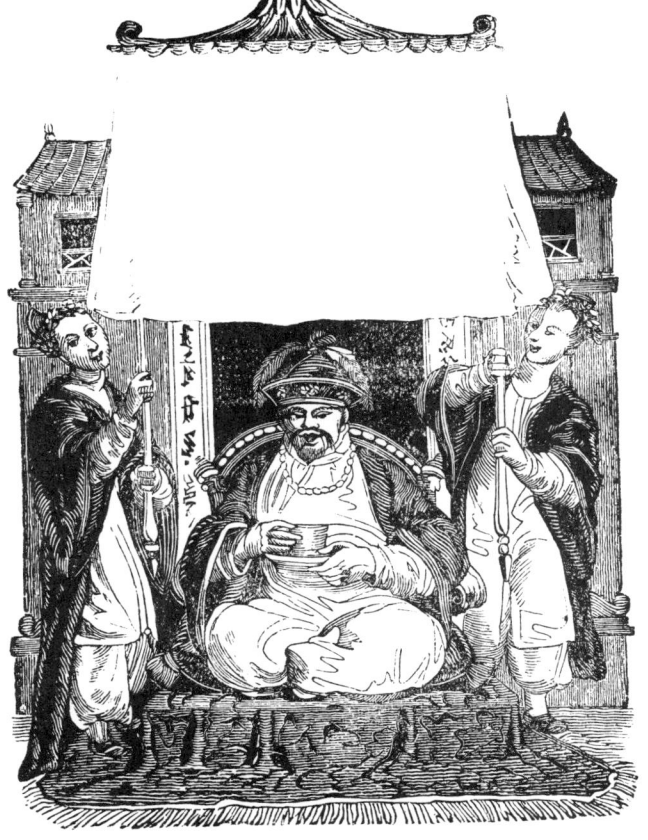

No. 75,—8s.

No. 76,—8s.

No. 77,—7s. 6d.

No 78,—8s.

No. 79,—6s.

No. 80,—8s.

No. 81,—6s.

No. 82,—8s.

No. 83,—7s. 6d.

No. 84,—8s.

No. 85,—6s.

No. 86,—7s. 6d.

No. 87,—7s.

No. 88,—9s. 6d.

No. 89,—3s. 6d.

No. 90,—15s.

No. 91,—9s. 6d.

No. 92,—*5s. 6d.*

No. 93,—*5s. 6d.*

No. 94,—*5s. 6d.*

No. 95,—*5s. 6d.*

No. 96,—*5s. 6d.*

No. 97,—*5s. 6d.*

No. 98,—6s. 6d.

No. 99,—6s. 6d.

No. 100,—6s. 6d.

No. 101,—6s. 6d.

No. 102,—6s. 6d.

No. 103,—6s. 6d.

No. 104,—10s.

Wᵐ MARKHAM

No. 105,—2s.

No. 106,—7s.

No. 107,—4s

No. 108,—3s.

No. 109,—6s.

No. 110,—5s.

No. 111,—4s.

No. 112,—5s.

No. 113,—4s.

No. 114,—4s. 6d.

No. 115,—6s.

No. 116,—3s.

No. 117,—4s. 6d.

No. 118,—2s. 6d.

No. 119,—3s. 6d.

No. 120,—2s. 6d.

No. 121,—2s.

No. 122,—3s.

No. 123,—7s.

No. 124,—5s.

No. 125,—2s. 6d.

No. 126,—1s. 6d.

No. 127,—3s.

No. 128,—7s.

No. 129,—6s.

No. 130,—4s.

No. 131,—3s.

No. 132,—2s.

No. 133,—3s. 6d.

No. 135,—7s.

No. 134,—17s. 6d.

TO BE SOLD BY AUCTION

TO BE SOLD

TO BE SOLD BY AUCTION

To be sold by Auction

TO BE SOLD BY AUCTION

No. 142,—7s. 6d.

No. 143,—8s.

No. 144,—6s.

No. 145,—6s.

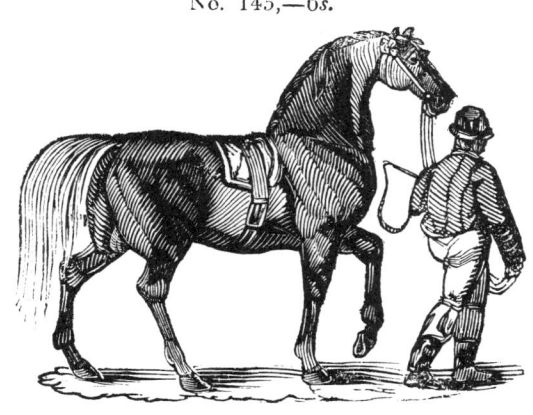

No. 146,—2s.

No. 147,—2s. 6d.

No. 148,—3s.

No. 149,—5s.

No. 150,—4s. 6d.

No. 151,—15s.

No. 152,—12s. 6d.

No. 153,—11s.

No. 154,—15s.

No. 155,—3s.

No. 156,—7s. 6d.

No. 157,—5s.

No. 158,—6s.

No. 159,—5s.

No. 160,—6s. 6d.

No. 161,—5s.

No. 162,—3s. 6d.

No. 163,—2s.

No. 164,—2s. 6d.

No. 165,—3s.

No. 166,—2s. 6d.

No. 167,—3s.

No. 168,—2s. 6d.

No. 169,—4s.

No. 170.—4s.

No. 171,—3s.

No. 172,—3s.

No. 173,—3s.

No. 174,—4s.

No. 175,—3s.

No. 176,—3s. 6d.

No. 177,—2s. 6d.

No. 178,—3s. 6d.

No. 179,—3s.

No. 180,—4s.

No. 181,—3s.

No. 182,—4s.

No. 183,—4s.

No. 184,—4s.

No. 185,—3s. 6d

No. 186,—2s.

No. 187,—3s.

No. 188,—4s.

No. 189,—4s.

No. 190,—4s. 6d.

No. 191,—4s.

No. 192,—4s.

No. 193,—4s.

No. 194,—3s. 6d.

No. 195,—3s.

No. 196,—3s.

No. 197,—3s. 6d.

No. 198,—3s.

No. 199,—4s.

No. 200,—4s.

No. 201,—4s. 6d.

No. 202,—4s.

No. 203,—3s.

No. 204,—3s. 6d.

No. 205,—3s. 6d.

No. 206,—3s. 6d.

No. 207,—3s. 6d.

No. 208,—3s. 6d.

No. 209,—2s. 6d.

No. 210,—3s.

No. 211,—3s.

No. 212,—3s 6d.

No. 213,—2s. 6d.

No. 214,—3s.

No. 215,—4s.

No. 216,—1s.

No. 217,—3s.

No. 218,—4s.

No. 219,—3s.

No. 220.—3s. 6d.

No. 221,—4s.

No. 222,—3s.

No 223,—3s. 6d.

224,—1s.

No. 225,—1s.

No 226,—1s.

No. 227,—1s.

No. 228,—2s.

No. 229,—3s. 6d.

No. 230,—2s.

No. 231,—3s.

No. 232,—3s.

No. 233,—3s.

No. 234,—3s. 6d.

No. 235,—3s. 6d.

No. 236,—2s. 6d.

No. 237,—3s. 6d.

No. 238.—3s. 6d.

No. 239,—2s.

No. 240,—3s. 6d.

No. 241,—2s. 6d.

No 242,—2s.

No. 243,—2s. 6d.

No. 244,—2s.

No. 245,—3s. 6d.

No. 246,—2s.

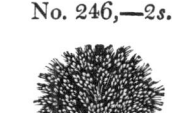

No. 247,—3s. 6d.

No. 248,—4s.

No. 249,—2s. 6d.

No. 250,—4s. 6d

No. 251,—4s.

No. 252,—4s.

No. 253,—4s.

No. 254,—4s.

No. 255,—4s.

No. 256,—4s.

No. 257,—4s.

No. 258,—4s.

No. 259,—4s.

No. 260,—4s.

No. 261,—4s.

No. 262,—4s.

No. 263,—4s.

No. 264,—4s.

No. 265,—4s.

No. 266,—4s.

No. 267,—1s.

No. 268,—4s.

No. 269,—*3s.*

No. 270,—*3s.*

No. 271,—*3s.*

No. 272,—*3s.*

No. 273,—*3s.*

No 274,—*3s.*

No. 275,—*5s. 6d.*

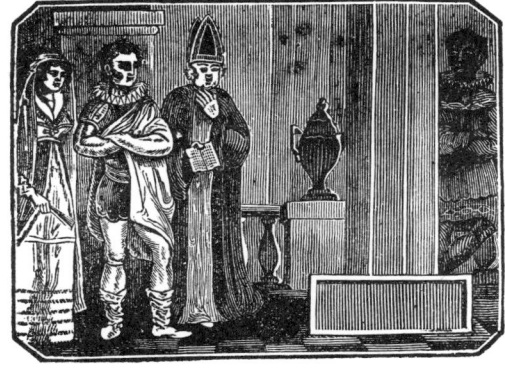

No 276,—*3s. 6d.*

No 277,—*3s.*

No. 278,—*2s.*

No 279,—*3s.*

No 280,—*2s. 6d.*

No. 281,—3s. 6d.

282,—4s]

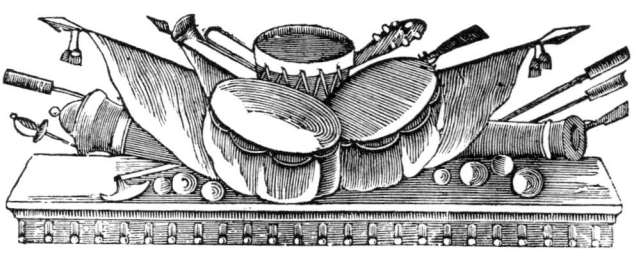

No. 283,—1s. 6d.

No. 284,—1s. 6d.

No. 285,—1s. 6d.

No. 286,—3s.

No. 287,—4s.

No. 288,—3s.

No. 289,—4s.

No. 290,—1s. 6d.

No. 291,—2s.

No. 292,—1s 6d.

No. 293,—2s.

No. 294,—1s.

No. 295,—3s.

No. 296,—1s. 6d.

No. 297,—3s.

No. 298,—3s.

No. 299,—1s. 6d.

No. 300,—3s.

No. 301,—2s. 6d.

No. 302,—2s.

No. 303,—1s.

No. 304,—3s.

No. 305,—2s.

No. 306,—2s. 6d.

No. 307,—1s. 6d.

No. 308,—3s.

No. 309,—2s.

No. 310,—2s. 6d.

No. 311,—2s.

No. 312,—1s. 6d.

No. 313,—2s.

No. 314,—5s. 6d.

No. 315,—4s. 6d.

No. 316,—4s. 6d.

No. 317,—3s.

No. 318,—1s. 6d.

No. 319,—2s. 6d.

No. 320,—2s.

No. 321,—2s.

No. 322,—1s. 6d.

No. 323,—1s. 6d.

No. 324,—2s.

No. 325,—2s. 6d.

No. 326,—3s.

No. 327,—1s. 6d.

No. 328,—1s. 6d.

No. 329,—2s.

No. 330,—9d.

No. 331,—1s.

No. 332,—1s. 6d.

No. 333—9d.

No. 334,—9d.

No 335,—1s. 6d.

No. 336,—1s. 9d.

No. 337,—3s.

No. 338,—2s. 6d.

No. 339,—2s. 6d.

No. 340,—2s. 6d.

No. 341,—3s.

No. 342,—2s. 6d.

No. 343,—1s. 9d.

No. 344,—3s.

No. 345,—2s.

No. 346,—4s.

No. 347,—2s.

No. 348,—2s.

No. 349,—1s. 6d.

No. 350,—1s.

No. 351,—1s.

No. 352,—2s.

No. 353,—1s. 6d.

No. 354,—1s. 6d.

No. 355,—2s. 6d.

No. 356,—1s.

No 357,—1s.

No. 358,—3s.

No. 359,—2s.

No. 360,—2s. 6d.

No. 361,—3s. 6d.

No. 362,—3s. 6d.

No. 363,—3s.

No. 364,—3s. 6d.

No. 365,—2s. 6d.

No. 366,—3s. 6d.

No. 367,—3s. 6d.

No. 368,—3s. 6d.

No. 369,—3s. 6d.

No. 370,—5s.

No. 371,—4s. 6d.

No. 372,—3s. 6d.

No. 373,—3s. 6d.

No. 374,—3s. 6d.

No. 375,—4s.

No. 376,—3s. 6d.

No. 377,—4s.

No. 378,—3s 6d.

No. 379,—3s. 6d.

No. 380,—3s. 6d.

No. 381,—3s. 6d.

No. 382,—3s. 6d.

No. 383,—3s. 6d

No. 284,—3s.

No. 385,—3s. 6d.

No. 386,—4s.

No. 387,—4s

No. 388,—3s. 6d.

No. 389,—3s. 6d.

No. 390,—4s.

No. 391,—3s. 6d.

No. 392,—4s. 6d.

No. 303,—3s.

No. 394,—3s. 6d.

No. 395,—3s. 6d.

No. 396,—3s. 6d.

No. 397,—4s.

No. 398,—3s. 6d.

No. 399,—3s. 6d.

No 400,—3s.

No. 401,—3s. 6d.

No. 402,—3s. 6d.

No. 403,—3s. 6d.

No. 404,—3s 6d.

No. 405,—4s. 6d.

No. 406,—4s. 6d.

No. 407.—4s.

No. 840,—*3s. 6d.* No. 409,—*3s. 6d.* No. 410,—*3s. 6d.*

No. 411,—*3s. 6d.* No. 412,—*3s. 6d.* No. 413,—*3s 6d.*

No. 414,—*3s.* No. 415,—*3s.* No 416,—*2s 6d.*

No. 417,—*3s. 6d.* No. 418,—*3s. 6d.* No 419,—*3s. 6d.*

No. 420,—*3s. 6d.* No. 421,—*3s. 6d.* No. 422,—*3s. 6d.*

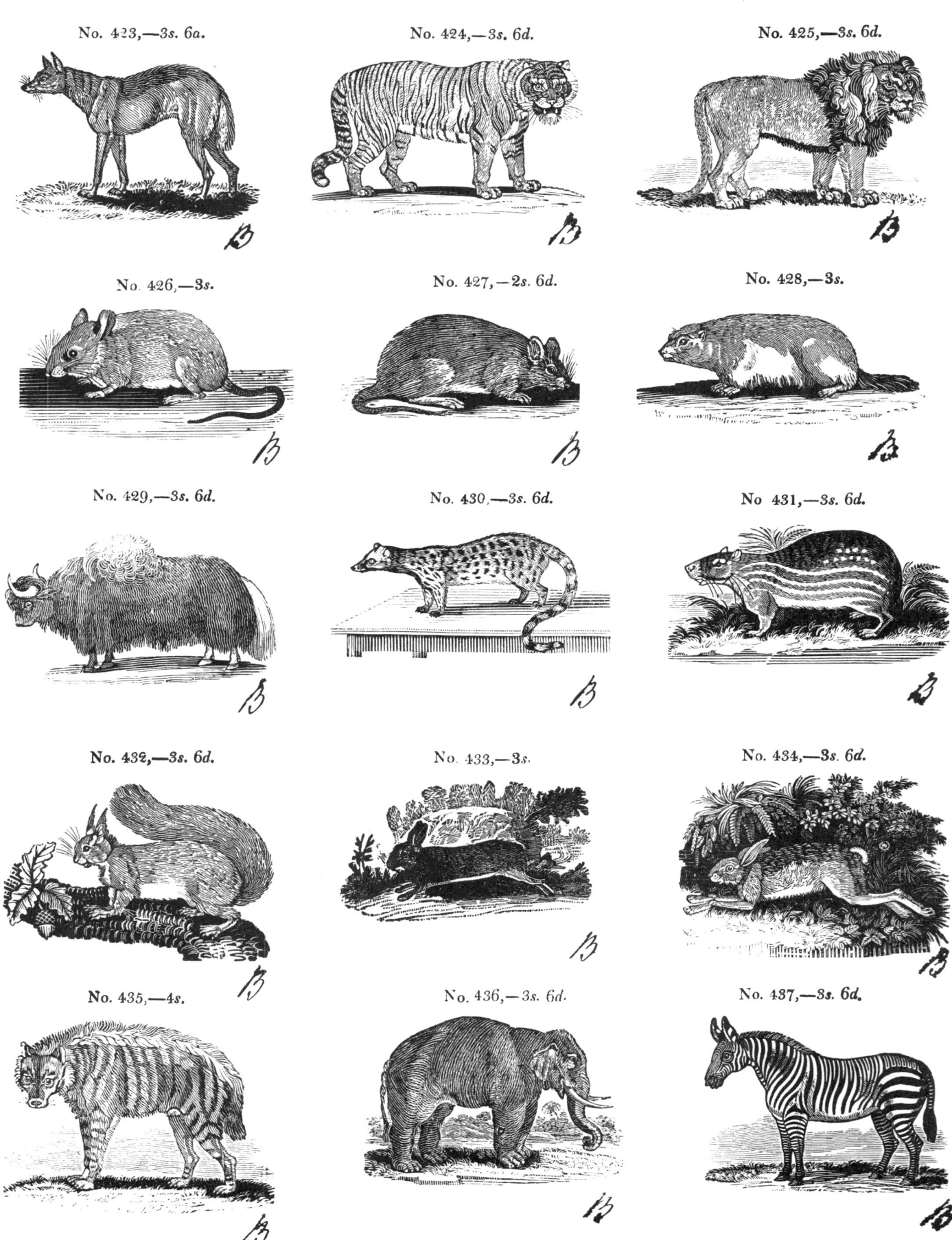

No. 423,—3s. 6a.

No. 424,—3s. 6d.

No. 425,—3s. 6d.

No. 426,—3s.

No. 427,—2s. 6d.

No. 428,—3s.

No. 429,—3s. 6d.

No. 430,—3s. 6d.

No 431,—3s. 6d.

No. 432,—3s. 6d.

No. 433,—3s.

No. 434,—3s. 6d.

No. 435,—4s.

No. 436,—3s. 6d.

No. 437,—3s. 6d.

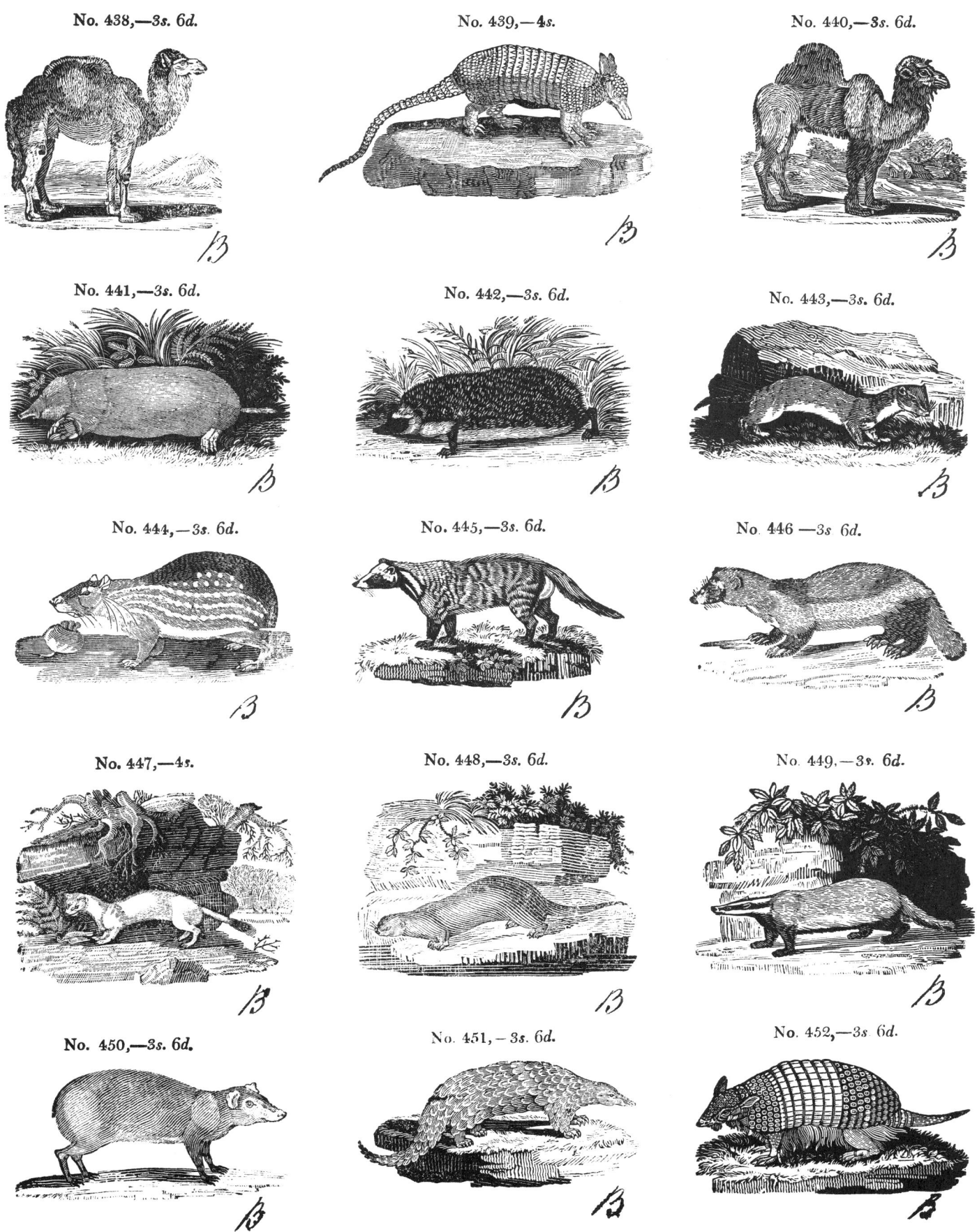

No. 438,—3s. 6d.

No. 439,—4s.

No. 440,—3s. 6d.

No. 441,—3s. 6d.

No. 442,—3s. 6d.

No. 443,—3s. 6d.

No. 444,—3s. 6d.

No. 445,—3s. 6d.

No. 446 —3s 6d.

No. 447,—4s.

No. 448,—3s. 6d.

No. 449,—3s. 6d.

No. 450,—3s. 6d.

No. 451,—3s. 6d.

No. 452,—3s 6d.

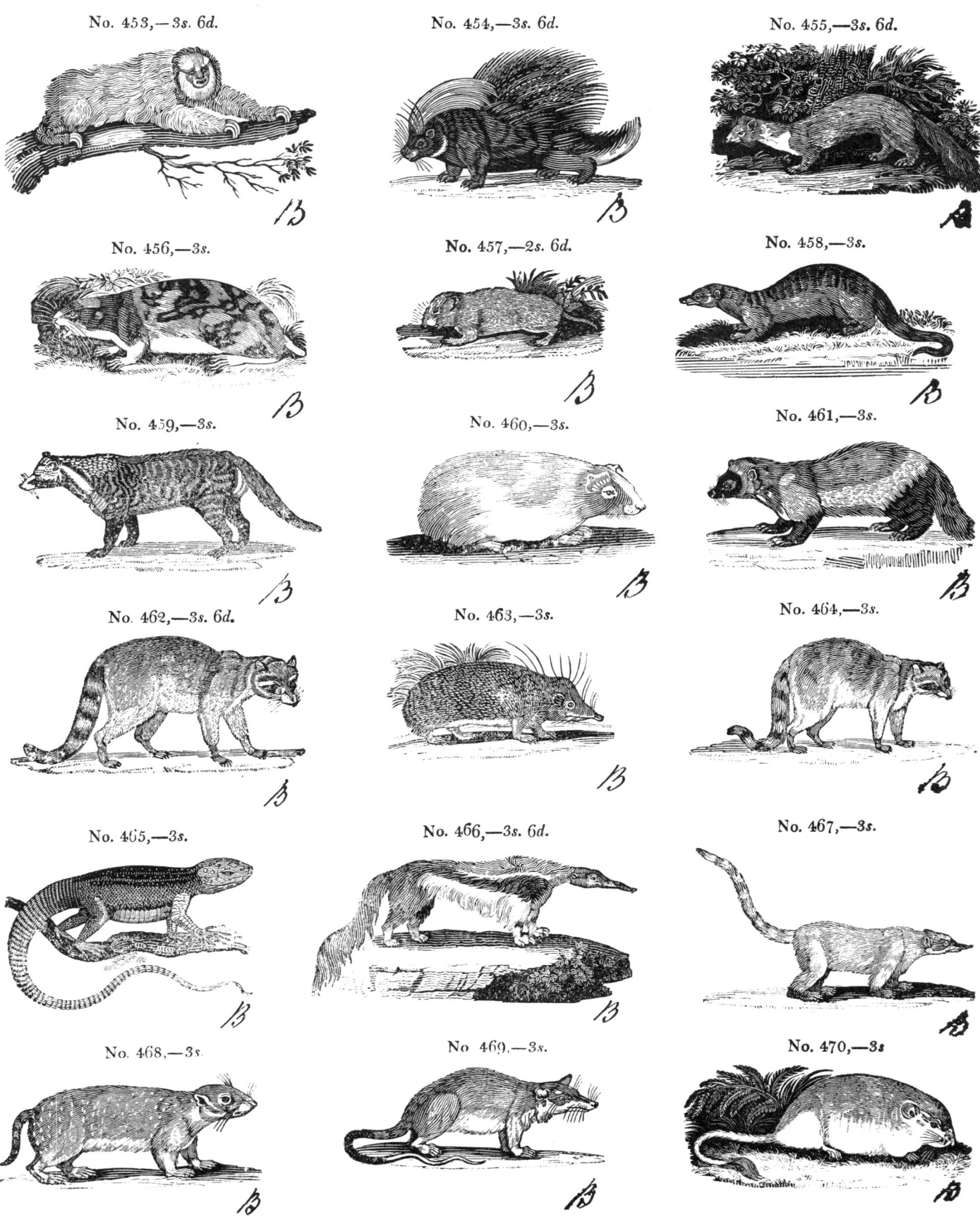

No. 453,—3s. 6d.

No. 454,—3s. 6d.

No. 455,—3s. 6d.

No. 456,—3s.

No. 457,—2s. 6d.

No. 458,—3s.

No. 459,—3s.

No. 460,—3s.

No. 461,—3s.

No. 462,—3s. 6d.

No. 463,—3s.

No. 464,—3s.

No. 465,—3s.

No. 466,—3s. 6d.

No. 467,—3s.

No. 468,—3s.

No. 469,—3s.

No. 470,—3s

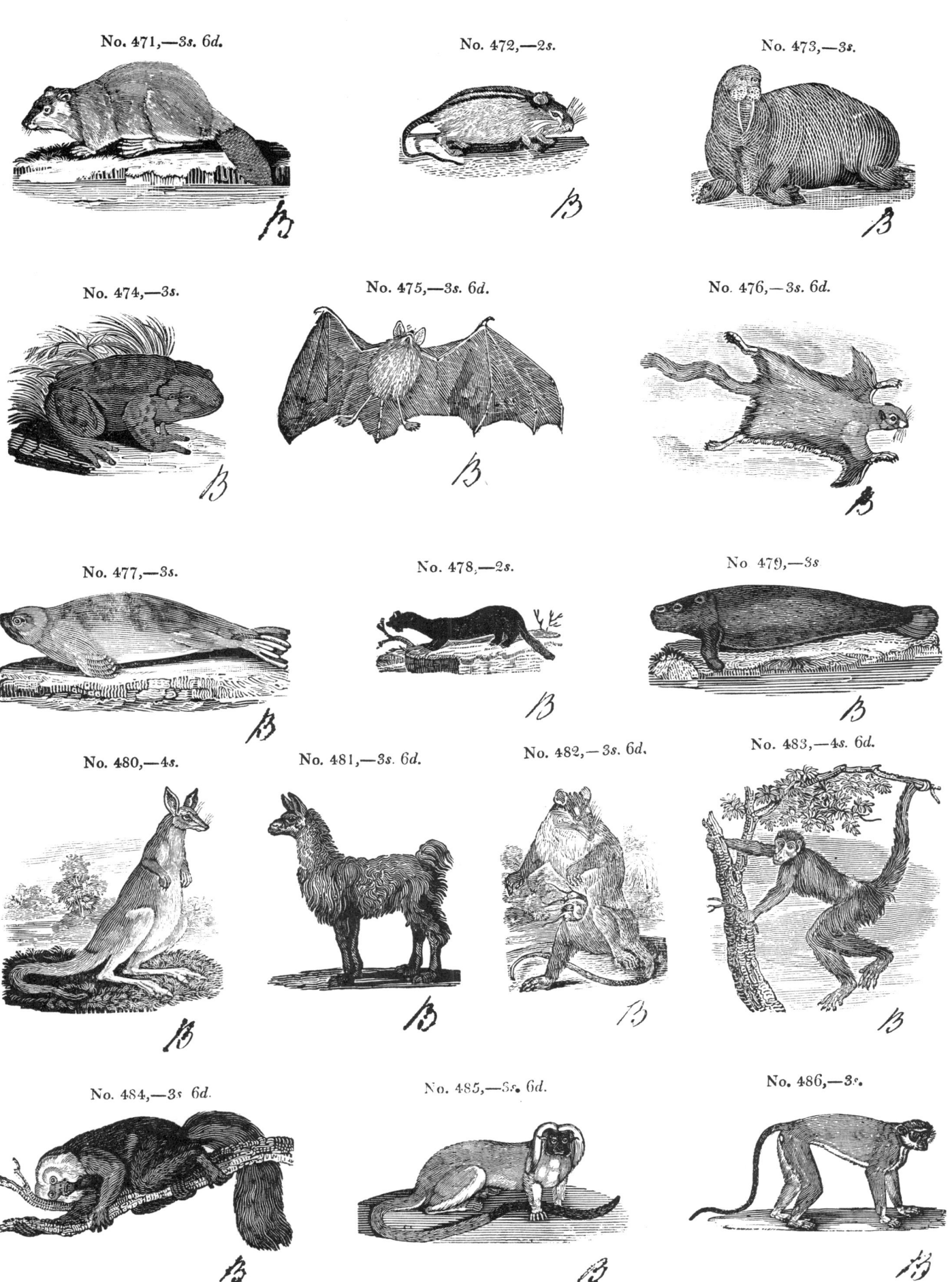

No. 471,—3s. 6d.

No. 472,—2s.

No. 473,—3s.

No. 474,—3s.

No. 475,—3s. 6d.

No. 476,—3s. 6d.

No. 477,—3s.

No. 478,—2s.

No 479,—3s

No. 480,—4s.

No. 481,—3s. 6d.

No. 482,—3s. 6d.

No. 483,—4s. 6d.

No. 484,—3s. 6d.

No. 485,—3s. 6d.

No. 486,—3s.

No. 487,—3s. 6d. No. 488,—3s. 6d. No. 489,—3s. 6d. No. 490,—3s. 6d. No. 491,—3s. 6d.

No. 492,—4s. No. 493,—3s. 6d. No. 494,—3s. 6d. No. 495,—4s.

No. 496,—3s. 6d. No. 497,—3s. 6d. No. 498,—3s. 6d.

No. 499,—3s. 6d. No. 500,—3s. 6d. No. 501,—3s. 6d.

No. 502,—3s. 6d.

No. 503,—3s. 6d.

No. 504,—3s. 6d.

No. 505,—4s.

No. 506,—3s. 6d.

No 507,—4s.

No. 508,—3s. 6d.

No. 509,—3s. 6d.

No. 510,—4s

No. 511,—4s.

No. 512,—3s. 6d.

No. 513,—3s. 6d.

No. 514,—3s. 6d.

No. 515,—3s. 6d.

No. 516,—4s.

No. 517,—4s. 6d.

No. 518,—4s.

No. 519,—4s.

No. 520,—4s.

No. 521,—4s.

No. 522,—4s.

No. 523,—4s.

No. 524,—3s. 6d.

No. 525,—4s.

No. 526,—3s. 6d.

No 527,—3s. 6d.

No. 528,—3s. 6d.　　　　No. 529,—4s.　　　　No. 530,—4s. 6d.

No. 531,—4s.　　　　No. 532,—4s.　　　　No. 533,—4s.

No. 534,—3s. 6d.　　　　No. 535,—3s.　　　　No. 536,—4s.

No 537,—3s. 6d.　　　　No. 538,　3s.　　　　No. 539,—3s.

No 540,—3s. 6d.

No. 541,—3s.

No. 542,—3s. 6d.

No. 543,—4s.

No 544,—4s.

No. 545,—4s.

No. 546,—3s. 6d.

No. 547,—4s.

No. 548,—4s.

No. 549,—4s.

No. 550,—3s. 6d.

No. 551,—3s. 6d.

No. 552,—4s.

No. 553,—3s.

No. 554,—2s. 6d.

No. 555,—*3s.*

No. 556,—*3s.*

No. 557,—*3s.*

No. 558,—*3s. 6d.*

No. 559,—*3s. 6d.*

No. 560,—*3s. 6d.*

No. 561,—*3s. 6d.*

No. 562,—*3s. 6d.*

No. 563,—*3s. 6d.*

No. 564,—*2s. 6d.*

No. 565,—*3s 6d.*

No. 566,—*3s 6d.*

No. 567,—*3s 6d.*

No. 568,—*3s. 6d.*

No. 569,—*3s. 6d.*

No. 570,—3s. 6d.

No. 571,—3s. 6d.

No. 572,—3s. 6d.

No. 573,—3s. 6d.

No. 574,—3s. 6d.

No. 575,—4s.

No. 576,—3s. 6d.

No. 577,—3s. 6d.

No. 578,—3s. 6d.

No. 579,—3s.

No. 580—3s.

No. 581,—3s.

No. 582,—3s. 6d.

No. 583,—3s. 6d.

No. 584,—3s. 6d.

No. 585,—3s. 6d.

No. 586,—3s. 6d.

No 587,—3s. 6d.

No. 588,—3s. 6d.

No. 589,—3s. 6d.

No. 590,—3s. 6a.

No. 591,—4s.

No. 592,—3s. 6d.

No. 593,—3s 6a.

No. 594,—4s.

No. 595 —4s. 6d.

No. 596,—4s.

No. 597,—3s 6d.

No. 598,—3s. 6d.

No 599 —3s.

No. 600,— 4s.   No. 601,— 4s.   No. 602,— 4s. 6d.

No. 603,— 3s. 6d   No. 604,— 4s.   No. 605,— 3s. 6d

No. 606 — 4s.   No. 607— 4s.   No. 608,— 4s.

No. 609.— 3s. 6d.   No. 610,— 3s. 6d.   No. 611,— 3s. 6d.

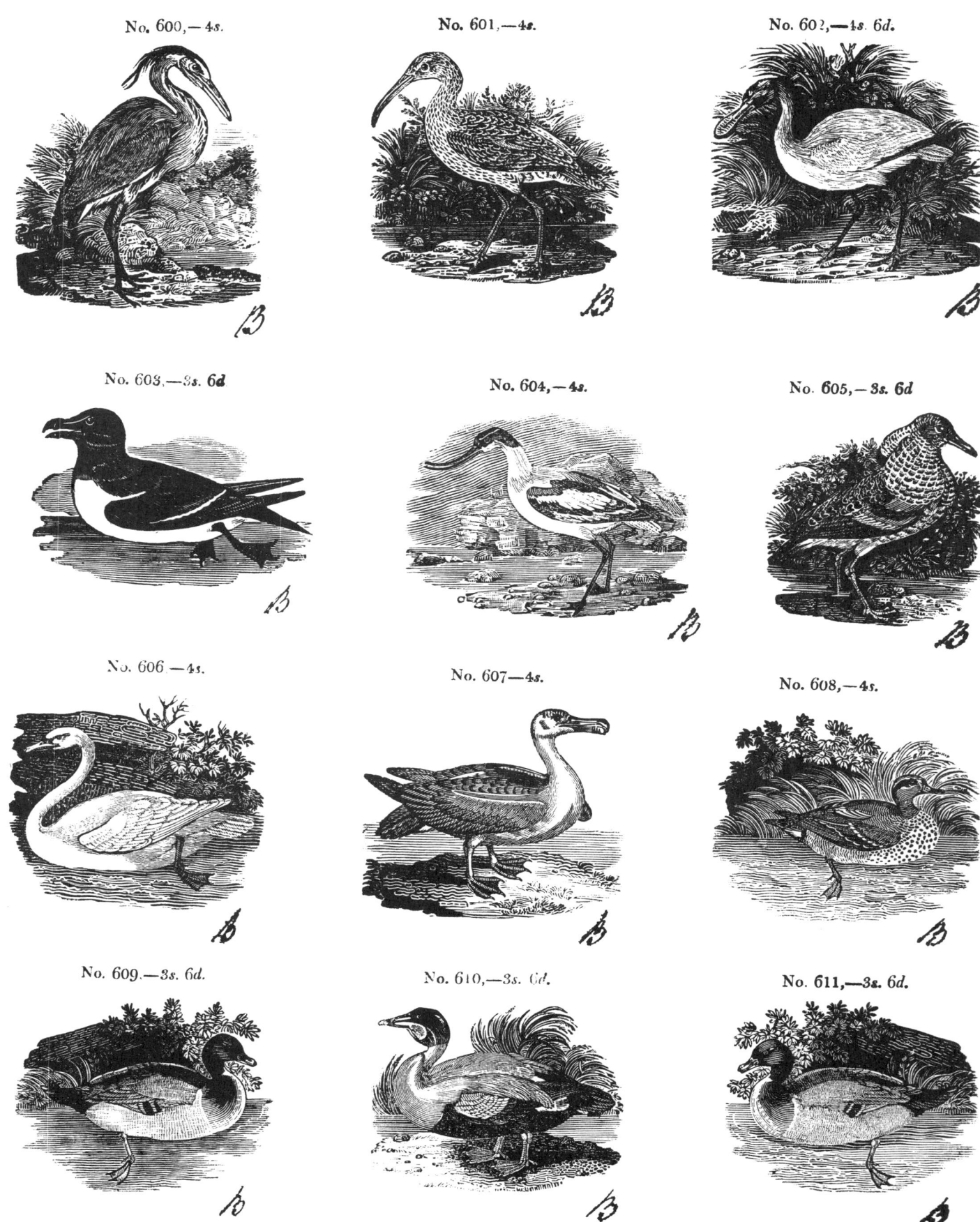

No. 612,—3s. 6d.

No. 613, – 3s. 6d.

No. 614,—3s. 6d.

No. 615,—3s. 6d.

No. 616,—3s. 6d.

No. 617,—3s. 6d.

No. 618,—4s.

No. 619,—3s. 6d

No. 620,—3s. 6d.

No. 621,—3s. 6d.

No. 622,—3s.

No. 623,—3s. 6d.

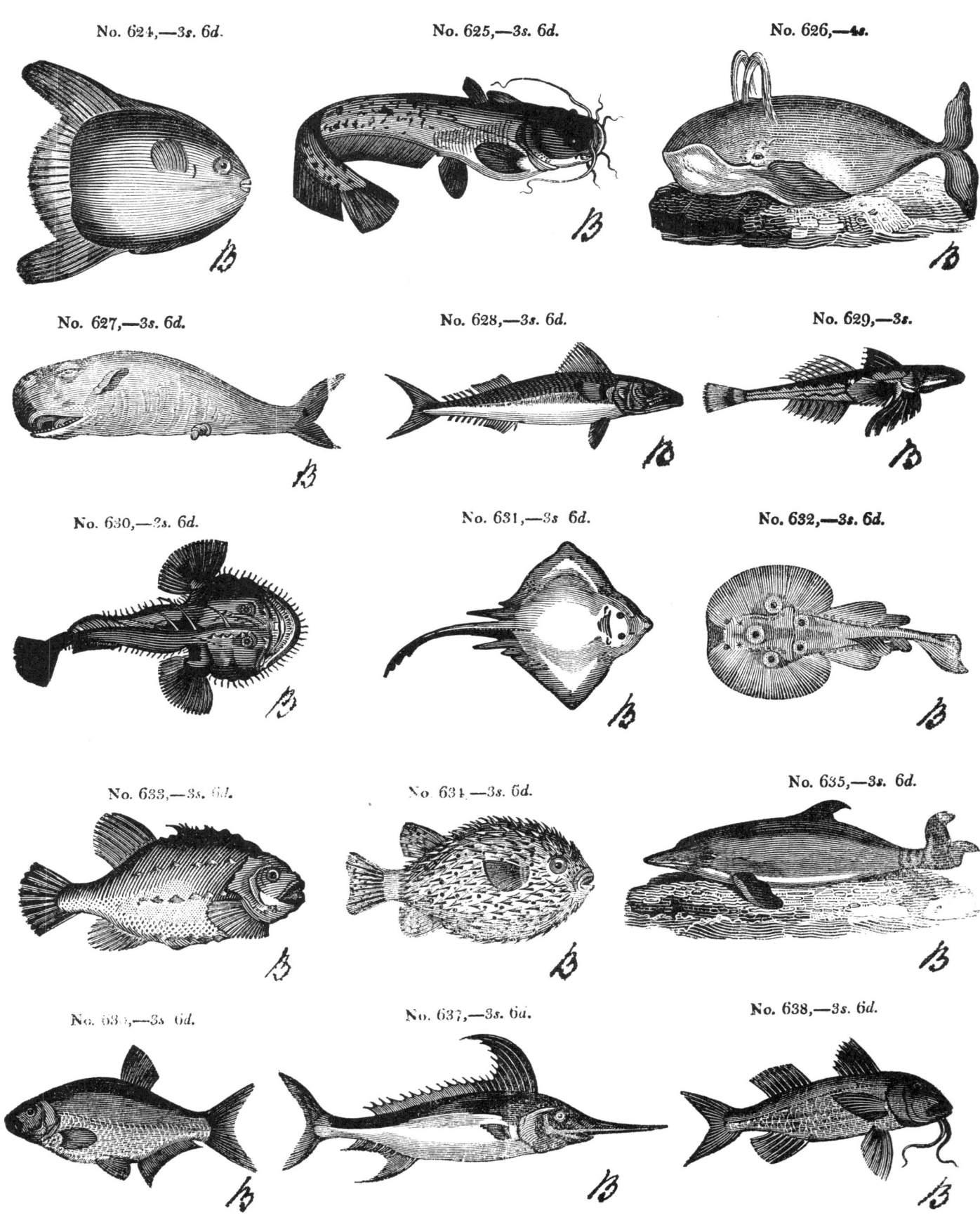

No. 624,—3s. 6d.

No. 625,—3s. 6d.

No. 626,—4s.

No. 627,—3s. 6d.

No. 628,—3s. 6d.

No. 629,—3s.

No. 630,—2s. 6d.

No. 631,—3s 6d.

No. 632,—3s. 6d.

No. 633,—3s. 6d.

No. 634,—3s. 6d.

No. 635,—3s. 6d.

No. 636,—3s 6d.

No. 637,—3s. 6d.

No. 638,—3s. 6d.

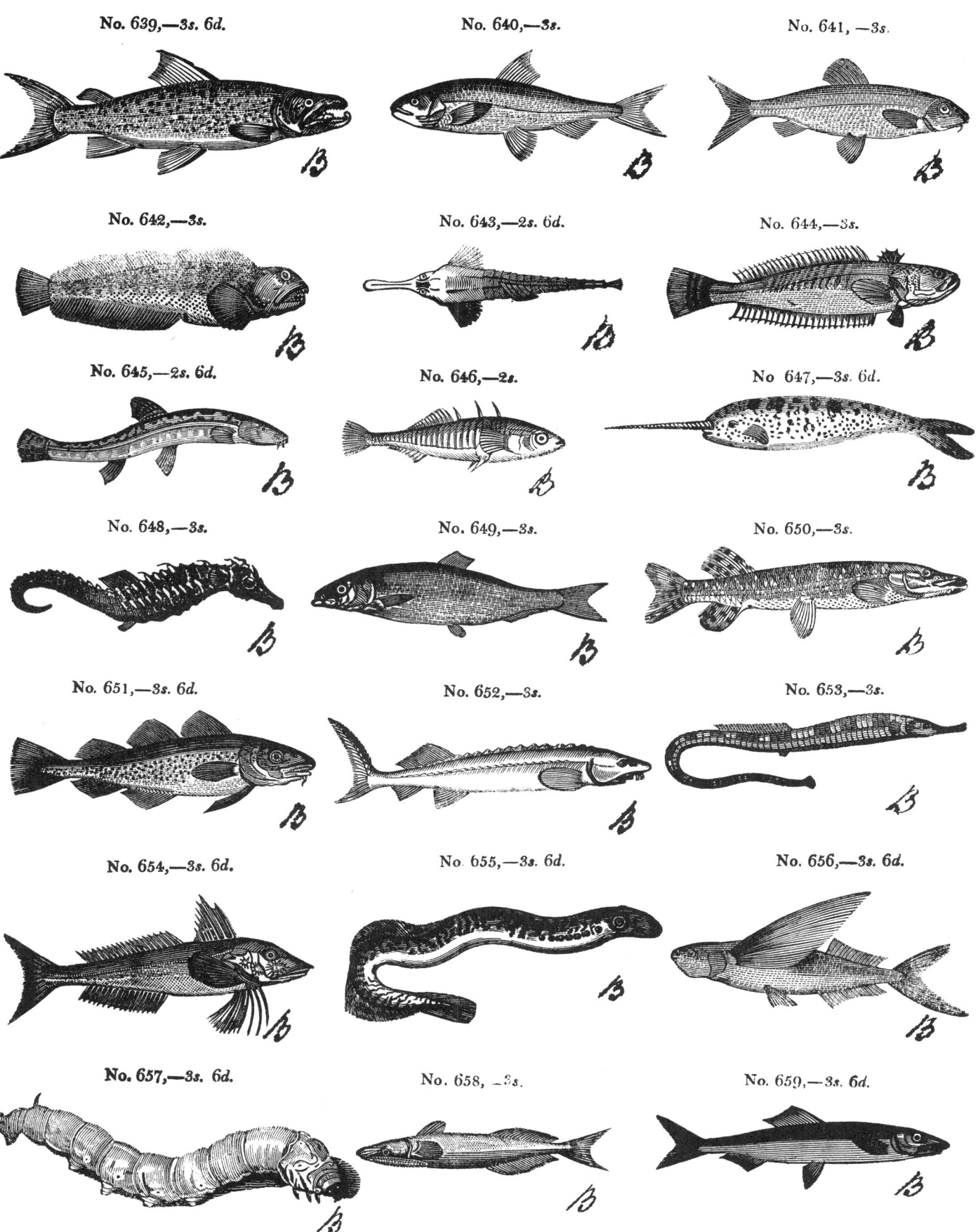

No. 639,—3s. 6d.

No. 640,—3s.

No. 641, —3s.

No. 642,—3s.

No. 643,—2s. 6d.

No. 644,—3s.

No. 645,—2s. 6d.

No. 646,—2s.

No 647,—3s. 6d.

No. 648,—3s.

No. 649,—3s.

No. 650,—3s.

No. 651,—3s. 6d.

No. 652,—3s.

No. 653,—3s.

No. 654,—3s. 6d.

No. 655,—3s. 6d.

No. 656,—3s. 6d.

No. 657,—3s. 6d.

No. 658, —3s.

No. 659,—3s. 6d.

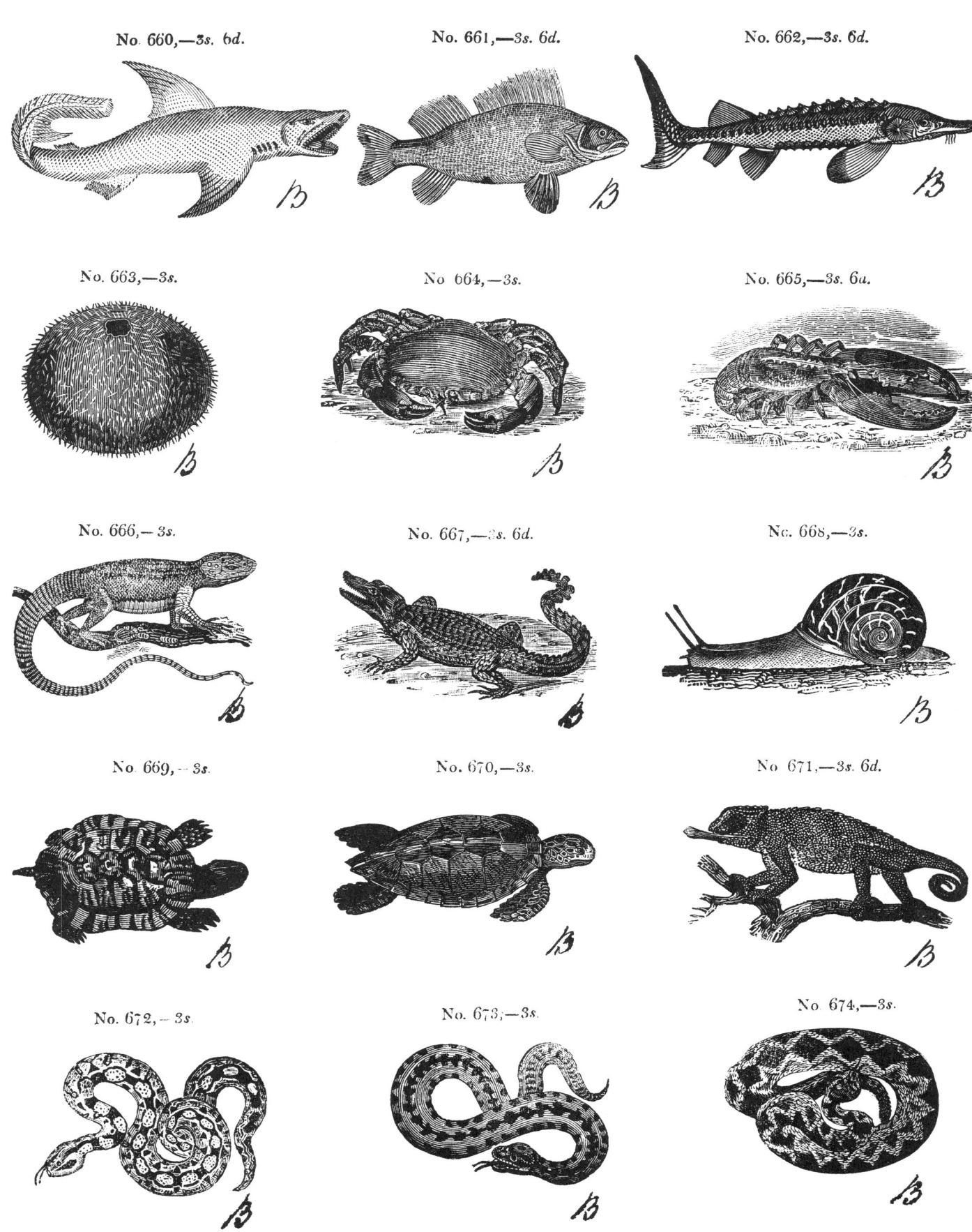

No. 660,—3s. 6d.   No. 661,—3s. 6d.   No. 662,—3s. 6d.

No. 663,—3s.   No 664,—3s.   No. 665,—3s. 6a.

No. 666,—3s.   No. 667,—3s. 6d.   Nc. 668,—3s.

No. 669,—3s.   No. 670,—3s.   No 671,—3s. 6d.

No. 672,—3s.   No. 673,—3s.   No. 674,—3s.

No. 675,—**3s.**

No. 676,—**3s.**

No. 677,—**3s.**

No. 678,—**3s. 6d.**

No. 679,—**3s. 6d.**

Nc. 680,—**3s. 6d.**

No. 681,—**3s. 6d.**

No. 682,—**3s.**

No. 683,—**3s. 6d.**

No. 684,—**3s. 6d.**

No. 685,—**3s.**

No. 686,—**3s. 6d.**

No. 687,—**1s.**

No. 688,—**1s. 6d.**

No. 689,—**1s. 6d.**

No. 690,—**1s.**

No. 691,—**1s 6a·**

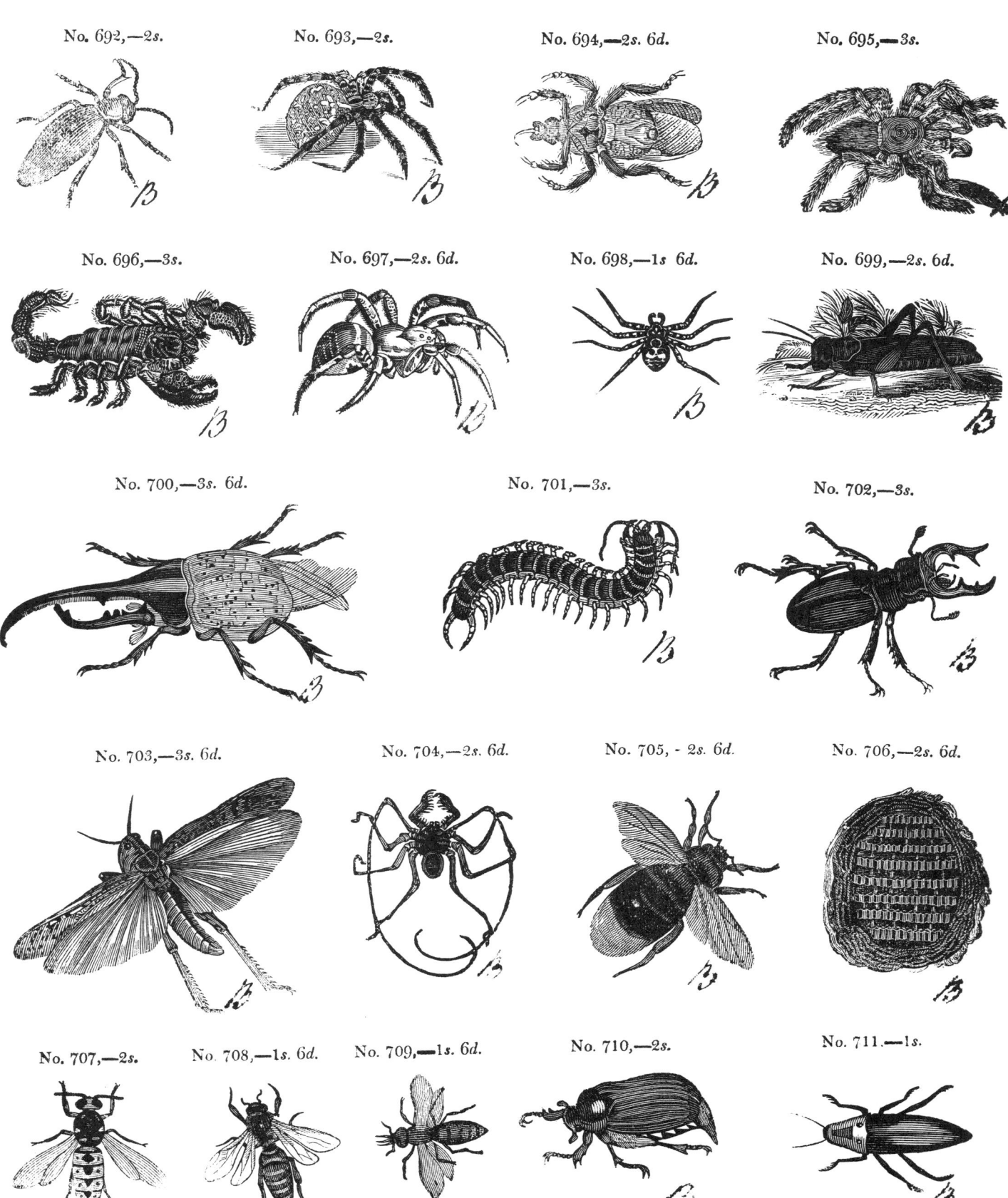

No. 692,—2s.

No. 693,—2s.

No. 694,—2s. 6d.

No. 695,—3s.

No. 696,—3s.

No. 697,—2s. 6d.

No. 698,—1s 6d.

No. 699,—2s. 6d.

No. 700,—3s. 6d.

No. 701,—3s.

No. 702,—3s.

No. 703,—3s. 6d.

No. 704,—2s. 6d.

No. 705, - 2s. 6d.

No. 706,—2s. 6d.

No. 707,—2s.

No. 708,—1s. 6d.

No. 709,—1s. 6d.

No. 710,—2s.

No. 711.—1s.

No. 712,—1s. 8d.   No. 713,—1s. 6d.   No. 714,—2s.   No. 715,—2s.

No. 716,—2s. 6d.   No. 717,—2s. 4d.   No. 718,—2s. 4d.   No. 719,—2s. 6d.

No. 720,—1s. 6d.   No. 721,—1s. 6d.   No. 722,—1s. 6d.   No. 723,—1s. 6d.

No. 724,—1s. 3d.   No. 725,—1s. 6d.   No. 726,—1s. 3d.   No. 727,—1s. 3d.

No. 728,—1s. 6d.   No. 729,—1s. 6d.   No. 730,—1s. 6d.   No. 731,—1s. 6d.

No 732,—1s. 6d.   No. 733,—1s. 6d.   No 734 —'s. 6d.   No 735,—1s. 6d.

No. 736,—1s. 6d.
No. 737,—1s. 6d.
No. 738,—1s. 6d.
No. 739,—1s. 6d.
No. 740,—1s. 6d.

No. 741,—1s. 6d.
No. 742,—1s. 6d.
No. 743,—1s. 6d.
No. 744,—1s. 6d.
No. 745,—1s. 6d.

No. 746,—1s. 6d.
No. 747,—1s. 6d.
No. 748,—1s. 6d.
No. 749,—1s.

No. 750,—2s. 6d.
No. 751,—1s. 6d.
No. 752,—2s. 6d.
No. 753, - 3s.

No. 754,—2s. 6d.
No. 755,—2s. 6d.
No. 756,—2s. 6d.

No. 757,—2s.

No. 758,—2s.

No. 759,—2s.

No. 760,—2s. 6d.

No. 761,—3s.

No. 762,—2s. 6d.

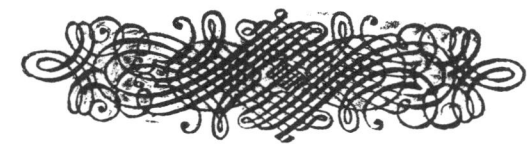

No. 763,—3s. 6d.

No. 765,—7s.

No. 766,—2s. 6d.

No. 767,—1s. 9d.

No. 764,—1s. 6d.

No. 768,—1s.

No. 769,—1s.

No. 770,—2s.

No. 771,—1s. 6d.

No. 772 —'s 9d.

No. 773,—2s. 6d.

No. 774,—3s.

No. 775,—2s. 6d.

No. 776,—2s. 6d.

No. 777,—3s. 6d.

No. 779,—7s. 6d.

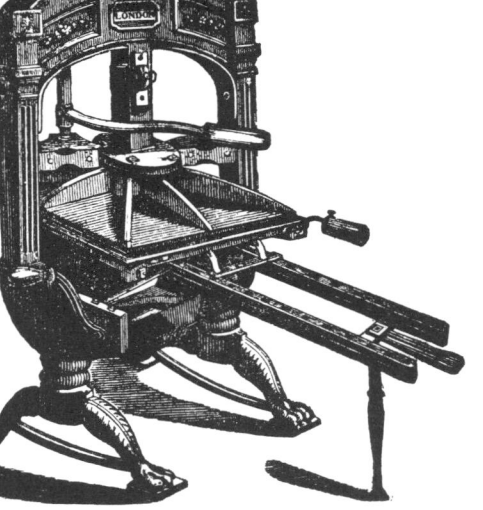

No. 780,—4s.

No. 778,—3s.

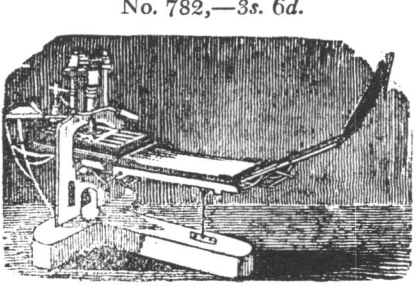

No. 781,—3s. 6d.

No. 782,—3s. 6d.

No. 783,—4s.

No. 784,—2s.

No. 785,—2s.

No. 786,—3s.

No. 787,—3s.

No. 788,—3s.

No. 789,—4s.

No. 790,—3s.

No. 791,—3s.

No. 792,—13s.

No 793,—5s. 6d.

No. 794,—6s.

No. 795,—4s. 6d.

No. 796,—5s.

No. 797,—6s.

No. 798,—5s.

No. 799,—3s.

No. 800,—3s. 6d.

No. 801,—3s.

No. 802,—1s. 9d.

No. 803,—3s.

No. 804,—3s.

No. 805,—1s. 6d

No. 806,—1s. 6d.

No. 807,—1s. 6d.

No. 808,—2s.

No. 809,—10s.

No. 810,—2s.

No. 811,—2s.

No. 812,—7s. 6d.

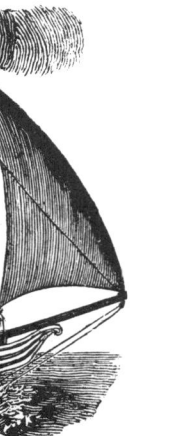

No. 813,—2s. 6d.

No. 814,— 2s. 6d.

No. 815,— 3s. 6d.

No. 816,—2s. 6d.

No 817,—3s.

No. 818,—2s. 6d.

No. 819,—2s. 6d.

No. 820,—2s. 6d.

No. 821,—2s. 6d.

No. 822,—2s. 6d.

No. 823,—2s. 6d.

No. 824,—3s.

No. 825,—2s.

No. 826,—3s.

No. 827,—10s. 6d.

No. 828,—2s.

No. 829,—2s. 6d.

No. 830,—10s. 6d.

No. 831, —5s 6d.

No. 832,—12s.

No. 833,—5s. 6d.

No. 834,—10s. 6d.

No. 835,—2s.

No. 836,—2s.

No. 837,—10s. 6d.

No. 838,—3s. 6d.

No. 839,— 9s. 6d.

No. 840,—4s. 6d.

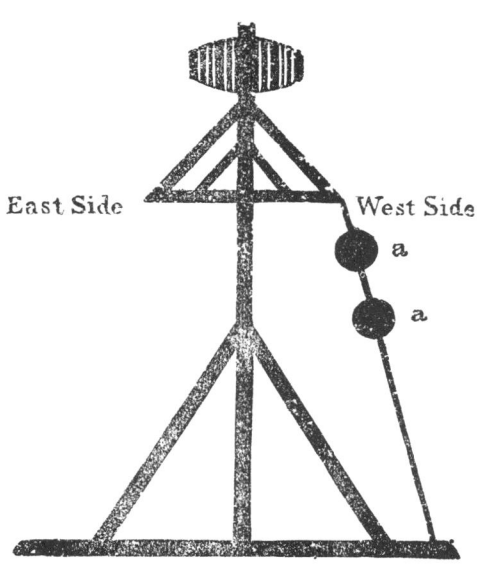

East Side   West Side

No. 841,—. 6d.

No. 842,—7s. 6d.

No. 845, —10s. 6d.

No. 846,—10s. 6d.

No. 847,—6s. 6d.

No. 848,—4s. 6d.

No. 849, —11s. 6d.

No. 850,—10s. 6d.

No. 851,—10s. 6d.

No. 852,—10s. 6d.

No. 853,—9s. 6d.

No. 854,—9s. 6d.

No. 855,—14s. 6d.

No. 856,—9s. 6d.

No. 857,—4s. 6d.

No. 858,—9s. 6d.

No. 859,—7s. 6d.

No. 860,—5s. 6d.

No. 861,—6s. 6a.

No. 862,—7s.

No. 863,—9s.

No. 866,—7s.

No. 864,   9s. 6d.

No. 867,—7s. 6d.

No. 865,—5s. 6d.

No. 868,—8s. 6d.

No. 871,—7s.

No. 869,—10s.

No. 870,—8s. 6d.

No. 872,—7s. 6d.

No. 873,—10s. 6d.

No. 874,—4s. 6d.

No. 875, —7s. 6d.

No. 876,—5s.

No. 877,—8s. 6d.

No. 878.—5s.

No. 879,—9s. 6d.

No. 880,—5s.

No. 881,—7s. 6d.

No. 882,—4s. 6d.

No. 883,—7s. 6d.

No. 884,—7s. 6d.

No. 885,—6s. 6d.

No. 886,—10s. 6d.

No. 887,—10s. 6d

No. 888,—3s 6d.

No. 889,—4s.

No. 890,—4s.

No. 891,—6s. 6d.

No. 892,—4s. 6d.

No. 893, —7s. 6d.

No. 894,—4s. 6d.

No. 898,—5s. 6d.

No. 899,—6s. 6d.

No. 900,—8s. 6d.

No. 901,—4s. 6d.

No. 902,—4s.

No. 903,—3s. 6d.

No. 904,—7s. 6d.

No. 905,—3s. 6d.

No. 906,—3s. 6d.

No. 907,—4s. 6d.

No. 908,—3s. 6d.

No. 909,—3s.

No. 910,—6s. 6d.

No. 911,—10s. 6d.

No. 912,—6s. 6d.

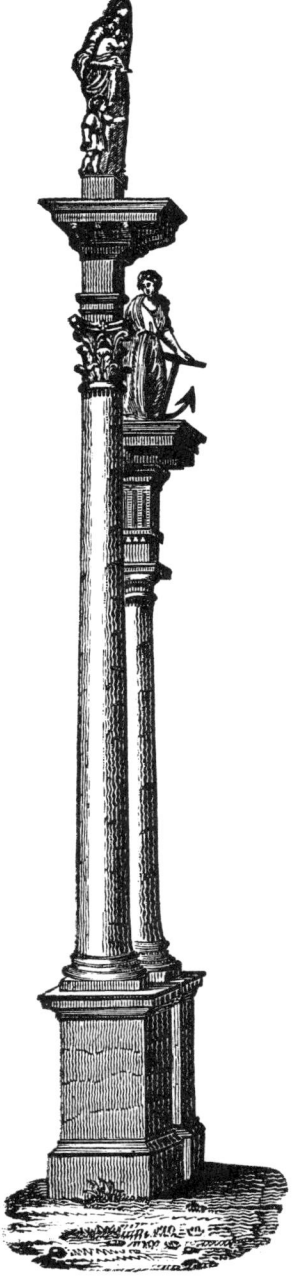

	£.	s.	D.
Breakfast with Eggs, &c.			
Lunch,			
Dinner and Dessert,			
Tea and Coffee,			
Supper,			
Wine,			
Brandy,			
Rum,			
Hollands,			
Cheerers and Negus,			
Ale and Porter,			
Whisky and Cider,			
Servant's Eating,			
Beds,			
Horses' Hay and Corn			
Blacksmith, &c.			

The above Cast is pierced, and the Name or any Sign may be inserted.

No. 913,—5s. 6d.

No. 914,—2s.

No. 915,—9s. the Set of six blocks.

No. 916,—3s.

Bought of

No. 917,—2s. 6d.

Grocer & Tea Dealer

No. 918,—3s.

Bought of

No. 919,—8s. 6d.

No. 920,—7s.

No. 921,—4s. 6d.

No. 922,—2s. 6d.

No. 923,—3s.

No. 924,—2s. 6d.

No. 925.

No. 926.

No. 927.

No. 928.

No. 929.

No. 930.

No. 931.

No 932.

No. 933.

No. 934.

No. 935.

No. 936.

No. 937.

No. 938.

No 939.

No. 940.

No. 941.

No 942.

No. 943.

No. 944.

No. 945.

No. 946.

No. 947.

No. 948.

No. 949.

No. 950

No. 951.

No. 952.

No. 953.

No. 954.

No. 955.

No. 956

No. 957.

No. 958.

No. 959.

No 960.

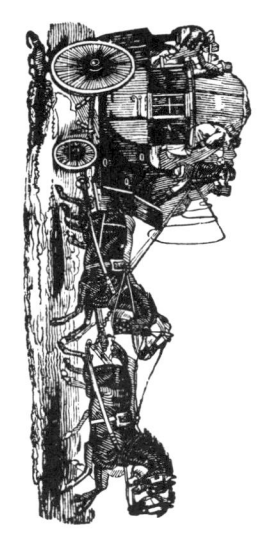

No. 962.

No. 963.

No. 964.

No. 961.

No. 965.

No. 966.

No. 967.

No. 968.

No. 969.

No. 970.

No. 971.

No. 972.

No. 973.

No. 974.

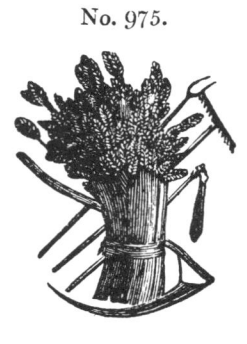

No. 975.

No. 976.

No. 977.

No. 979.

No. 980.

No. 981.

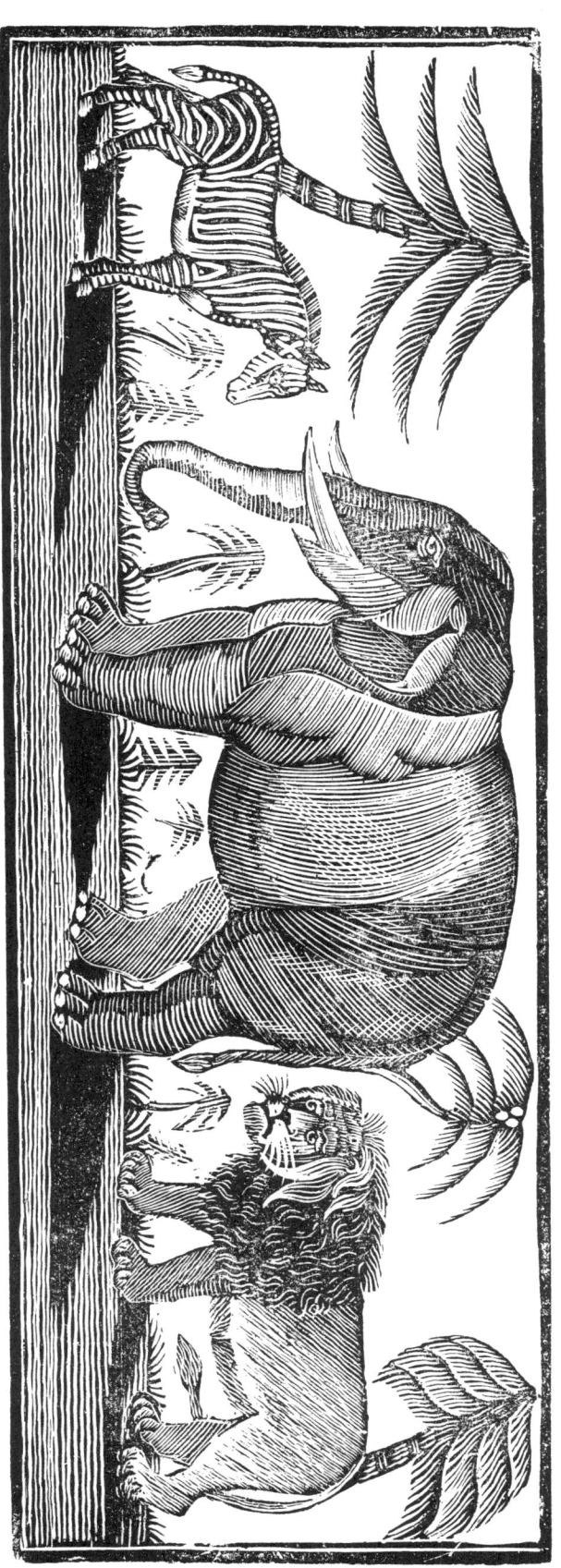

No. 978.

No. 984.

No. 985.

No. 986.

No. 987.

No. 988.

No. 989.

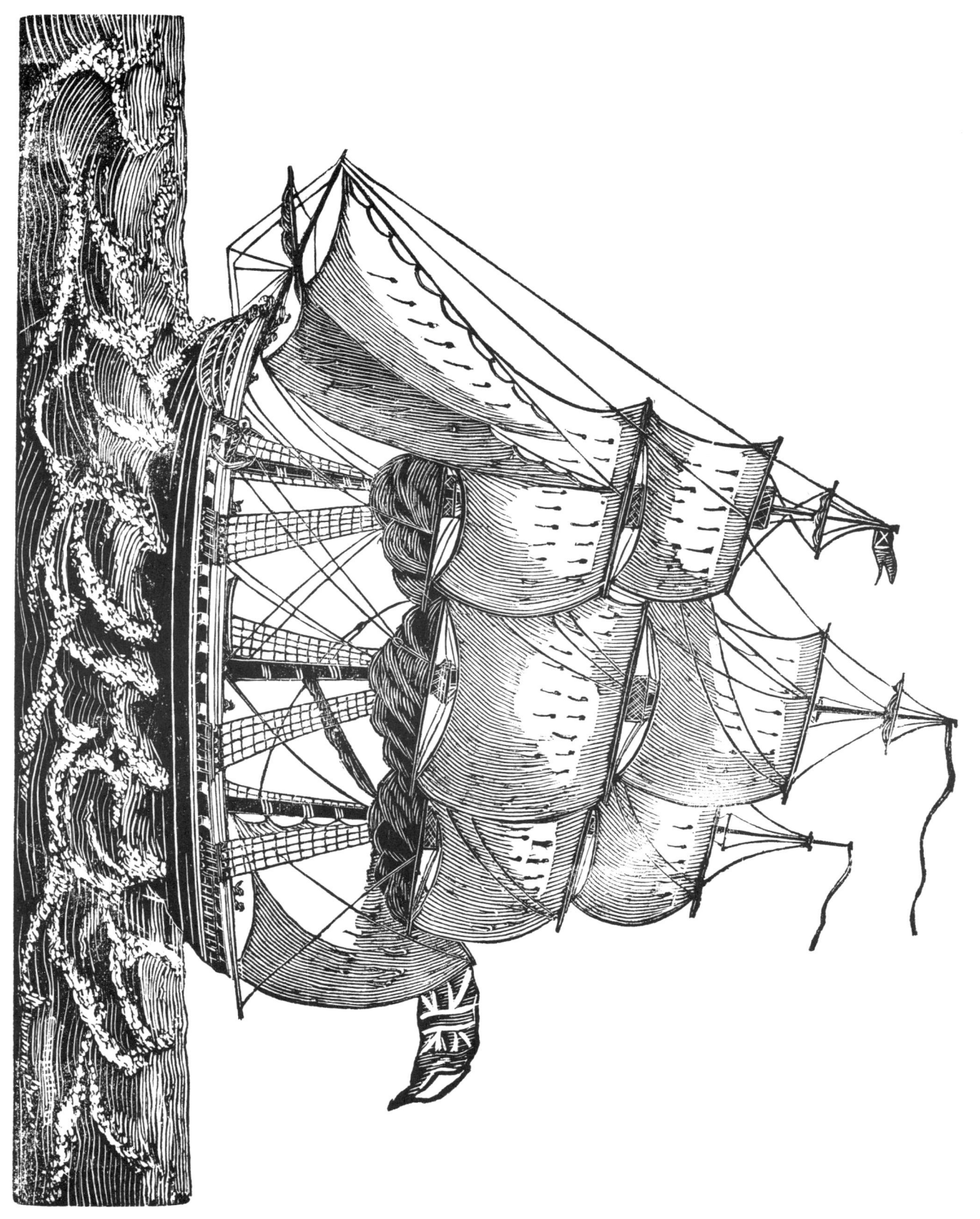

No. 990.

No. 991.

No. 992.

No. 993.

No. 994.

No. 995.

No. 996.

No. 997.

No. 998.

No. 999.

No. 1000.

No. 1001.

No 1002.

No. 1003.

No. 1004.

No. 1005.

No. 1006.

No. 1007.

No. 1008.

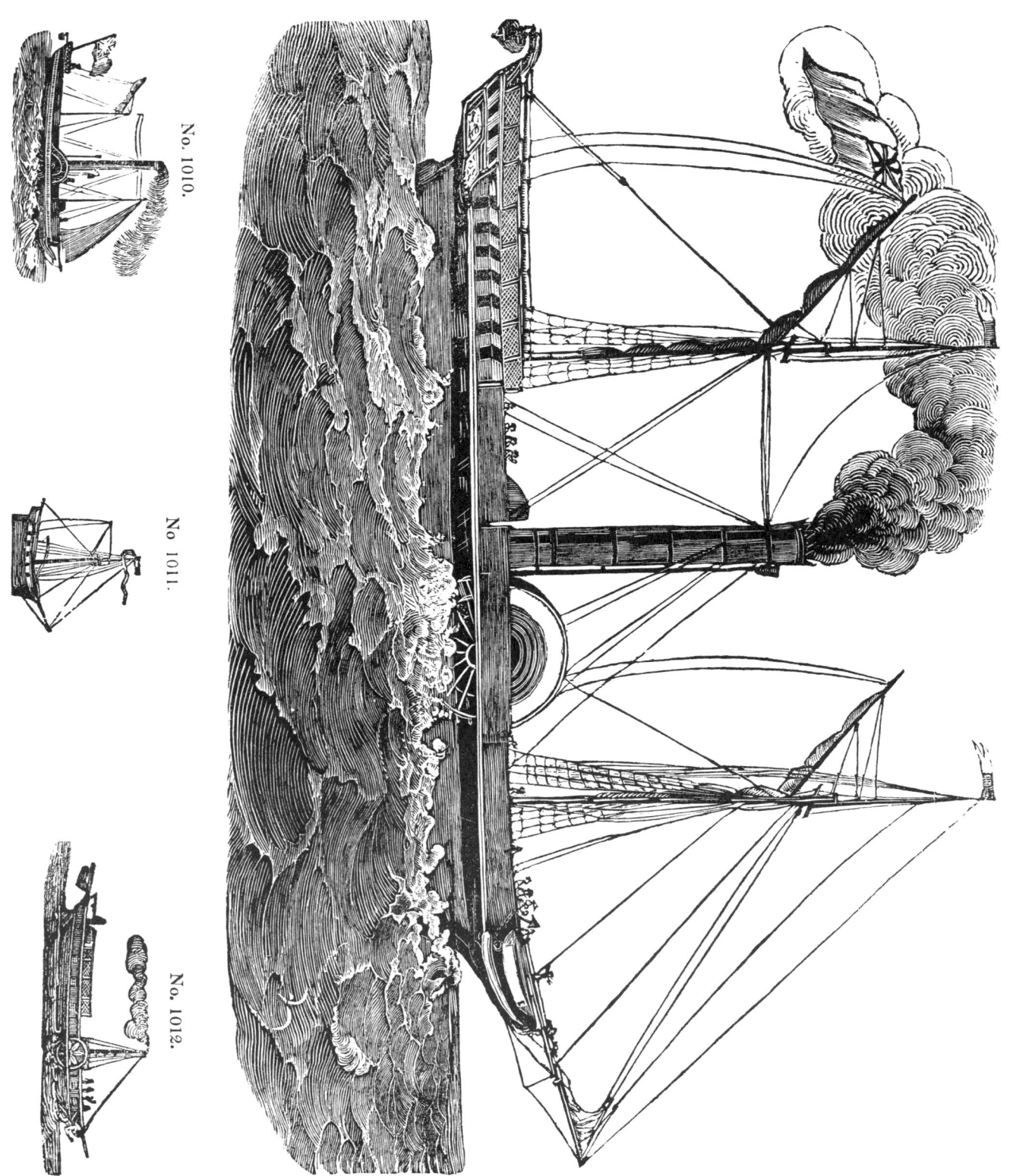

No. 1010.

No. 1011.

No. 1012.

No. 1009.

No. 1013.

No. 1014.

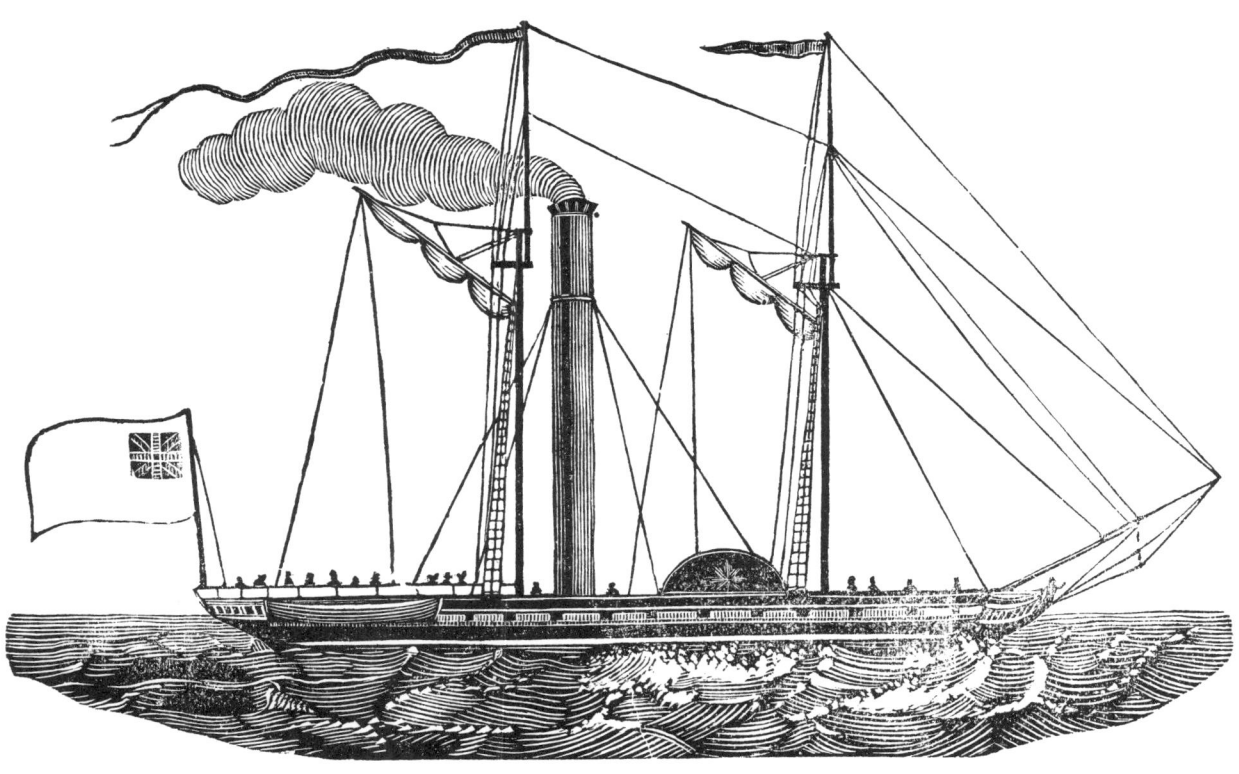

No. 1016.

No. 1018.

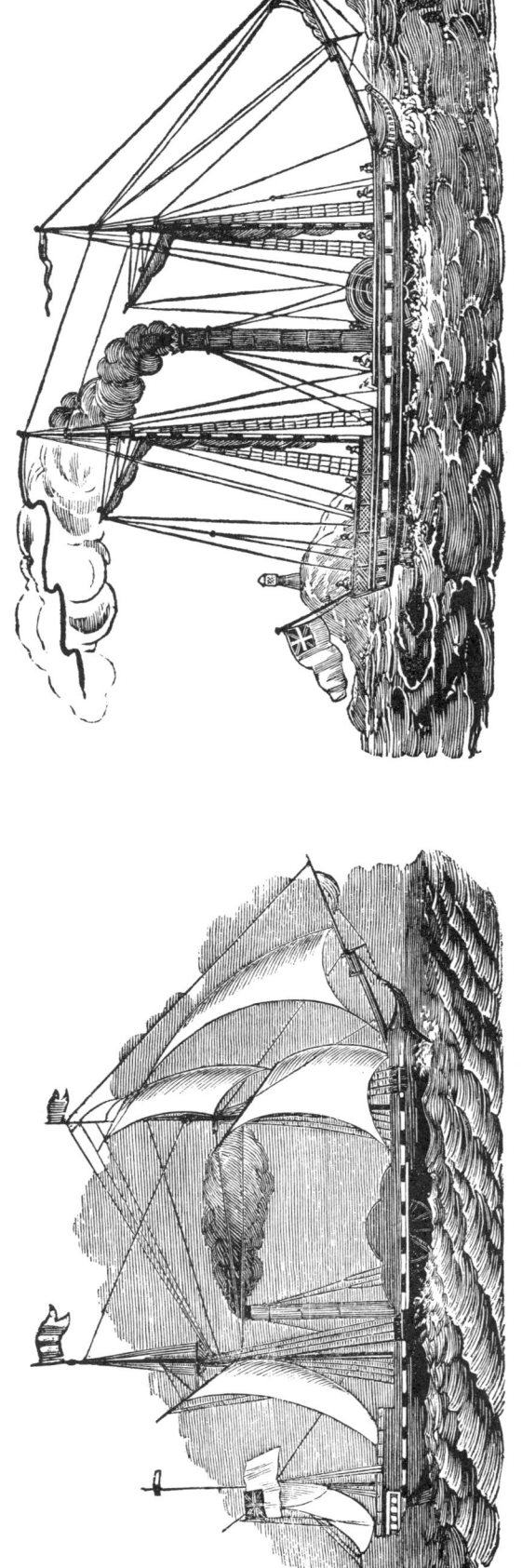

No. 1015.

No. 1017.

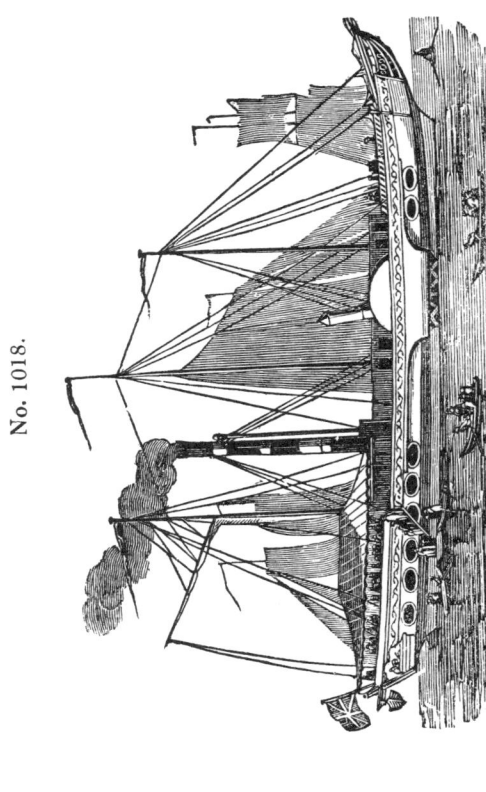

No. 1019.

No. 1020.

No. 1021.

No. 1022.

No. 1023.

No. 1024.

No. 1025.

No. 1026.

No. 1027.

No. 1028.

No. 1029.

No. 1030.

No. 1031.

No. 1032.

No. 1033.

No. 1034.

TEA, COFFEE AND SPICES.

No. 1035.

No. 1036.

No. 1037.

No. 1038.

No. 1039.

No. 1040.

No. 1041.

No. 1042.

No. 1043.

No. 1044.

No. 1045.

No. 1046.

No. 1047.

No. 1048.

No. 1049.

No. 1050.

No. 1051.

No. 1052.

No. 1053.

No. 1054.

No. 1055.

No. 1056.

No. 1057.

No. 1059.

No. 1060.

No. 1061.

No. 1062.

*Nos 1063-79 are missing
in this original and have not yet
been found in other copies.*

No. 1080.

No. 1081.

No. 1082.

No. 1083.

No. 1084.

No. 1085.

No. 1086.

No. 1087.

No. 1088.

No. 1089.

No. 1090.

No. 1091.

No. 1092.

No. 1093.

No. 1094.

No. 1095.

No. 1096.

No. 1097.

No. 1098.

No. 1098.

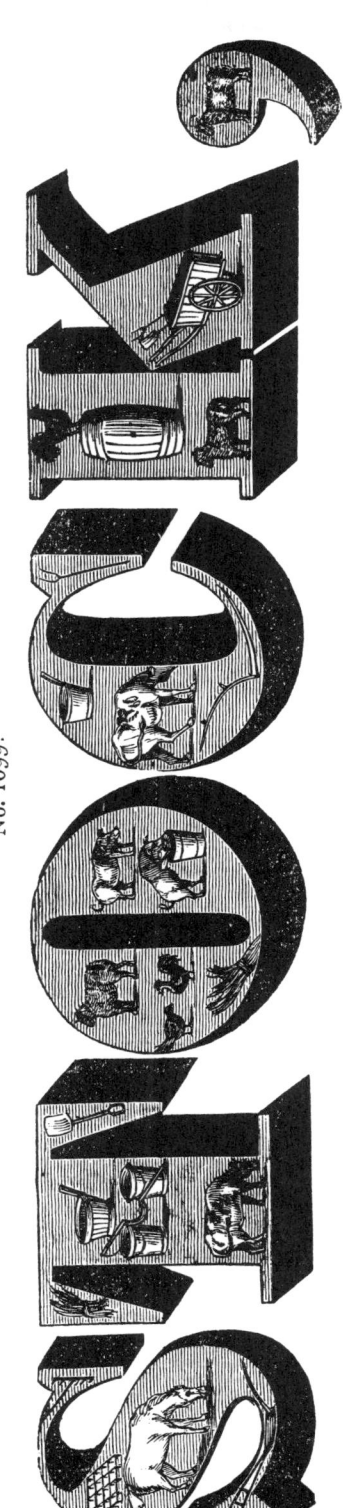

No. 1099.

No. 1100.

JOBBING SPECIMENS

500 April 1829

C. CARR,

BIRD AND BUSH, ELSDON.

	£.	s.	D.
Breakfast			
Lunch			
Dinner			
Supper			
Port			
Sherry and Shrub . .			
Lisbon, Claret, and Madeira .			
Cheerers and Negus . .			
Punch			
Brandy, Rum, and Gin .			
Whisky			
Coffee and Tea . .			
Ale and Porter . .			
Servants' Eating and Ale .			
Paper, Pipes and Tobacco .			
Beds and Bed-room Fires .			
Horses' Hay and Corn .			
Blacksmith . . .			
Grass and Turnips . .			
Greasing and Hostler . .			

£

WILLIAM GRAHAM,

ALNWICK & NEWCASTLE CARRIER,

BEGS leave to return his grateful acknowledgments to his Friends and the Public for the preference that has invariably been given to him in carriage to and from the above places, and trusts, that, from the attention which will continue to be paid to their commands, he will merit their future favours.

W. G. Begs also to state that he leaves Alnwick for Newcastle every Monday, Wednesday, and Thursday; and Newcastle for Alnwick every Tuesday, Thursday, and Friday; and that the following are the present rates of Carriage to Merchants.

Wheat 9d. per Boll
Bale Goods 2d. per Stone
Dry Goods in Proportion
Wool Packs 3s.—Pack Weight.

Alnwick, April 28th, 1817.

Davison, Printer, Alnwick.

A PLEASURE TRIP

TO THE

FARN ISLANDS,

On SUNDAY, July 14th, 1839.

The Wansbeck

Will leave **WARKWORTH** Harbour at 5 o'Clock in the Morning, calling at **ALNMOUTH** at 6 o'Clock, and will return the same Evening. Every attention will be paid to the accommodation of Passengers.

☞ Fares **2s.** each.

WILLIAM BLAKEY, MASTER.

DAVISON, PRINTER, ALNWICK.

C. PEAREY,
DEALER IN GENUINE
TEAS, COFFEES, &c.
BRANTON.

JOHN FRENCH,
BLACK AND WHITE SMITH,
MACHINE MAKER, &c.

GREEN BAT, ALNWICK,

RETURNS thanks to the Farming Gentlemen for the numerous Orders he has received during the time he has conducted the above Business; and having made considerable Improvements in Drill Machines and other Agricultural Implements, he begs to assure them that every exertion on his part will be made to merit a continuance of their patronage.

J. F. begs to state, that all Orders with which he may be favoured will be executed with despatch, and warranted of the best materials and workmanship, at the following reduced Prices:—

	£	s.	d.
Common Swing Plough - - -	3	0	0
Ribbing Plough - - -	1	10	0
Cleaning Scuffler with 3 Hoes -	1	10	0
Double Mould-board Plough - -	3	0	0
Ditto with Scufflers to clean Drills -	3	10	0
Double Turnip Drill - - -	5	0	0
Single Turnip Drill - - -	1	15	0
Grubber with 8 Coulters and 4 Wheels	8	0	0
Whickening Brake with 2 Wheels -	3	10	0
Iron Haimes, made from 7s. per pair to	0	8	0

Machine for weighing Live Stock to any weight.
Iron Axles of all sizes.
Sledge Mells and Hammers of all kinds from 1 lb. to 30 lb.
Scale Beams made or repaired with the greatest accuracy.

Alnwick, May 1st, 1829.

DAVISON, PRINTER, ALNWICK.

To be Sold

BY AUCTION,

At Wreigh Hill,

IN THE PARISH OF ROTHBURY,

On SATURDAY the 6th of May, 1843,

W. DONKIN, AUCTIONEER,

ALL THE

STOCK

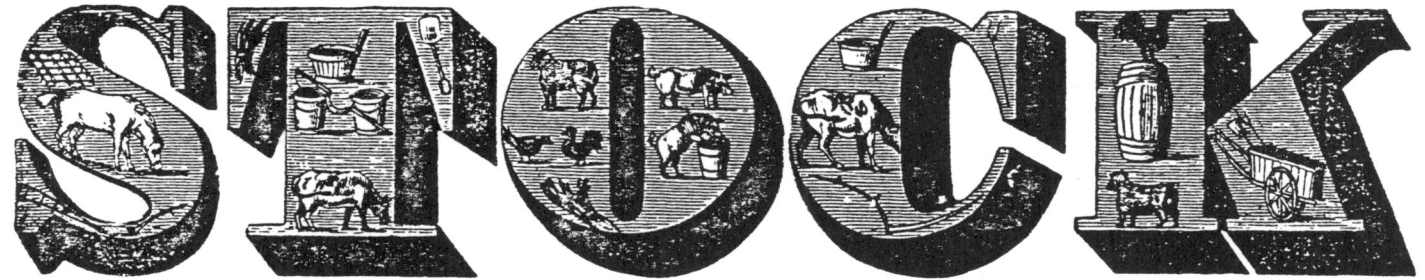

UPON THE SAID FARM,

Consisting of 46 Half-bred Ewes with their Lambs, 41 Half-bred Hogs, 1 Leicestershire Tup, 3 Milk Cows, calved and to calve, 1 Quey in Calf, 6 two-years-old Queys and Steers, 3 one-year-old Queys and Steers, 7 Draught Horses, 1 two-years-old Filly, 1 Sow and 8 Shots. Together with all the Carts, Ploughs, Harrows, and the Smaller Implements of Husbandry.

The Sale to begin at 2 o'Clock in the Afternoon.

Wreigh Hill, April, 1843.

DAVISON, PRINTER, ALNWICK.

W. DAVISON,

Chemist, Druggist, Apothecary, &c.

BONDGATE STREET, ALNWICK,

GRATEFUL to his Friends and the Public for the liberal Patronage with which he has uniformly been honoured since his establishment in Business in the year 1802, respectfully begs to state that it will ever be his study to merit a continuance of their distinguished support by a strict attention to their interests in always being furnished with an extensive Stock of Genuine Medicines direct from the Manufacturing Chemists and the most respectable Medical Establishments in London.

Pickles and Spices from Lazenby's and others.

India Curry Paste, Madras Mulligatawny, Bengal Chattny, and Chattny Sauce, &c. from the House of Bruce, Kennett, and Barrie, of Madras.

Patent Medicines, &c. from the respective Preparers.

Oils, Colours, Varnishes, Dyes, Painters' Brushes, &c. &c.

Newman's, Reeves', and other Manufacturers' prepared Colours; Drawing, Camel-Hair, Fitch, and other Pencils.

Cigars and Fancy Snuffs, from Taddy & Co., London.

Genuine Teas and Coffees.

Perfumery, Soaps, &c. from Rigge's, Berry's, Rowland's, Butler's, &c. &c. Foreign and English.

Some thousands of Volumes of new and scarce second-hand Books, at half the publishing Prices.

A great Variety of elegant Engravings, Fancy Prints, and Paintings, on the most moderate Terms.

WANTED AN APPRENTICE

To an Apothecary, &c. a steady Youth of respectable Connexions, who writes a good Hand, and understands Book-Keeping and Latin. A Premium will be required.

TO BE LET,

AND ENTERED TO IMMEDIATELY,

Two Convenient Dwelling Houses,

Pleasantly situated in the Green Bat Street, Alnwick. Also Two Rooms behind the same. Apply as above.

Alnwick, May, 1829.

Davison, Printer, Alnwick.